A Freudian Slip
Is When You
Say One Thing
but Mean
Your Mother

879 Funny, Funky, Hip, and Hilarious Puns

GARY BLAKE

Skyhorse Publishing

Skyhorse Publishing books may be purchased in bulk at special discounts for
sales promotion, corporate gifts, fund-raising, or educational purposes. Special
editions can also be created to specifications. For details, contact the Special
Sales Department, Skyhorse Publishing, 307 West 36th Street, 11th Floor,
New York, NY 10018 or info@skyhorsepublishing.com.

Skyhorse® and Skyhorse Publishing® are registered trademarks of Skyhorse
Publishing, Inc.®, a Delaware corporation.

Visit our website at www.skyhorsepublishing.com.

10 9 8 7 6 5 4 3 2 1

Library of Congress Cataloging-in-Publication Data

Blake, Gary.
 A Freudian slip is when you say one thing but mean your mother : 879 funny,
funky, hip, and hilarious puns / Gary Blake. -- 1st ed.
    p. cm.
 ISBN 1-61608-734-X (hardcover : alk. paper)
1. Puns and punning. 2. American wit and humor. I. Title.
PN6231.P8B74 1990
818'.5402--dc23

                        2012012555

ISBN: 978-1-61608-734-0

Printed in China

For Louise

Contents

Acknowledgments

I'D LIKE TO THANK my dog, without whom this book would never have been bitten.

Also, I am grateful for the person who wrote the enduring line, "And don't call me Shirley."

Finally, a big thank you to the folks at Skyhorse Publishing, who have given me more support than my Dr. Scholl's foot pads. My personal thanks to my long-time friend and colleague-in-punnery Steve Price, who encouraged me to write this book and kept me motivated long after I realized that writing hundreds of puns had permanently damaged my stem cells.

Introduction

LET US NOW PRAISE Famous Puns.

Puns are not the lowest form of humor; in fact, they may be the highest.

They certainly have a fine provenance: from the Bible, Chaucer, Pope, Shakespeare, Rabelais, Tolstoy, Joyce, Lewis Carroll, John Donne, Oscar Wilde, Nabokov, and Beckett to the movie *Airplane!*—"And don't call me Shirley!"

A biblical pun is found in Matthew 16:18: "Thou art Peter and upon this rock I will build my church." The Greek name for Peter, which also means "stone," is quite close to the Greek word for "rock."

Dryden called puns the "lowest and most groveling kind of wit." To Ambrose Bierce, puns were a "form of wit to which wise men stoop and fools aspire."

Shakespeare couldn't resist a pun, such as this from *Richard III* ("Now is the winter of our discontent/Made glorious summer by the sun of York"), in which he puns on sun and son. *Romeo and Juliet* is filled with puns. In *Julius Caesar*, there is a cobbler who, when asked what he does, replies, "I am a mender of men's soles" (souls). Samuel Johnson disparaged Shakespeare for his puns, calling puns "the lowest form of humor."

Lewis Carroll tossed off puns in *Alice In Wonderland*, such as:

> "And how many hours a day did you do lessons?" said Alice, in a hurry to change the subject.
>
> "Ten hours the first day," said the Mock Turtle, "nine the next, and so on."
>
> "What a curious plan!" exclaimed Alice.
>
> "That's the reason they're called lessons," the Gryphon remarked, "because they lessen from day to day."

The curmudgeonly comic Oscar Levant famously opined that "a pun is the lowest form of humor—unless you think of it first." It seems like we must first disapprove a pun instead of laugh at it. To paraphrase Rodney Dangerfield, "Puns don't get no respect."

The tradition of wordplay can be traced back thousands of years and, in the United States, we are surrounded by puns that are good, bad, and sometimes ugly. There are stores at the mall that rely on puns to communicate their business idea (an optometrist's store is "A Site for Sore Eyes"), films from The Marx Brothers to *Airplane!* to the OO7 films in which James Bond dispenses a pun whenever he prefers to be oblique. In *Moonraker*, Hugo Drax asks, "Why did you break up the encounter with my pet python?" Bond says, "I discovered it had a crush on me."

Comics like Steven Wright base their entire comic personas on existential interpretations of far-out puns (e.g., "I went to a general store. They wouldn't let me buy anything specifically."). Could *Tonight Show* host Jay Leno even exist without puns? "The teenage sex problem is mounting. Why? Do they keep on slipping off?" Abbott and Costello could milk a pun endlessly, as when Bud announced that he'd been hired at a bakery as a "loafer."

Newspapers like the *New York Post* (this headline when dancer Fred Astaire died: "Taps for Fred Astaire") and other tabloids would be lost without them (during a British heat wave: "London Broils"). The *New York Post*'s prize pun may have been "Headless Body Found in Topless Bar." Here's one that is quite possibly an urban legend but sticks in my mind nonetheless. It concerns an escaped patient from a secure ward at a psychiatric hospital who rapes two laundry workers and flees the scene—"Nut screws washers and bolts." I don't know if it was ever actually published, but "The Colonel Kicks the Bucket" went around a lot when Colonel Sanders died. Even World War II correspondents found solace in puns. When William Shirer went from Paris to the bureau of the Chicago Tribune Universal Service owned by William Randolph Hearst, he cracked, "I'm going from bad to Hearst."

It seems as though those who name their cabin cruisers ("Playbuoy," "Buoy Crazy," "Marlin Monroe") and racehorses ("Lady Leggs") cannot resist puns either, as any trip to a marina or a stable will confirm. And surfing the TV offerings will yield punny titles like *Taking Stock* (a financial show) and *Pawn Stars*, which I won't even go into. Ad slogans stick in the mind better when a pun is present ("Mumm's the Word"; from a cosmetics company: "Aging is history"). And then there's the classic ad for a French vermouth: "Don't Stir without Noilly Prat." These days, products on shelves form their own puns, like "Cherries Garcia," and then there are even stores like "Staples."

Friends thrived on puns, as did *Frasier* (*from the episode* "*Frasier* Has Spokane," Frasier: "That's perfect—Brian being a seismologist, and you having so many faults."), *Monk*, *How I Met Your Mother*, *Gilmore Girls* . . . and game shows like *Minute to Win It*.

Eighty years ago, wit, humor, and puns abounded at the Algonquin Round Table with George S. Kaufman's acerbic wit creating his own form of punning. (Round Table regular and theatre critic Alexander Woolcott's title for his review of theatrical plays was *Enchanted Aisles*.) Once, when Kauffman was stuck with a terrible bridge partner, the partner excused himself to urinate. Kaufmann, wearing his usual world-weary expression, said to the other two players: "This is the first time all evening I know what he has in his hand."

My favorite example of a political pun was said by Adlai Stevenson. It's a pun in which the sound of the words and the juxtaposition of ideas result in cleverness of a high order. Stevenson was asked his opinion of Pope Paul and of Norman Vincent Peale. He answered, "I find Paul appealing and Peale appalling."

When it comes to Broadway plays and musicals, puns are the hallmark of our wittiest and most popular writers. Cole Porter's "Brush Up Your Shakespeare" from *Kiss Me Kate* comes to mind. Each refrain of "Brush Up Your Shakespeare" includes at least one pun on the title of a Shakespeare play ("If she says your behavior is heinous/Kick her right in the *Coriolanus*.") In Sondheim's *Sweeney Todd*, a whole song about the types of people that will be ground up into Mrs. Lovett's pies is done in puns. Mr. Sondheim, in *Into the Woods*, tells us, in the "Jack and the Beanstalk" segment, that "the ends justify the beans." And we know from the song "Comedy Tonight" in *A Funny Thing Happened on the Way to the Forum* that "weighty affairs will just have to wait." Kander and Ebb's *Curtains* uses self-conscious puns ("Though an analyst may/Never couch it that way . . . ").

Playwright Neil Simon builds a marvelous wordplay in *The Odd Couple* when he has his sloppy character Oscar Madison confront his meticulous roommate Felix Ungar "I can't take it anymore, Felix, I'm cracking up. Everything you do irritates me. And when you're not here, the things I know you're gonna do when you come in irritate me. You leave me little notes on my pillow. Told you 158 times, I can't stand little notes on my pillow. 'We're all out of corn-flakes. F. U.' Took me three hours to figure out 'F. U.' was Felix Ungar!"

A century before Neil Simon, Gilbert and Sullivan exploited outrageous puns in *H. M. S. Pinafore* ("And that junior partnership, I ween, / Was the only ship that I ever had seen," said the First Lord of the Admiralty, Sir Joseph Porter). Also from *Pinafore*, "refrain, audacious tar, your suit from pressing." "Magnet Hung in a Hardware Store," from *Patience*, has a whole verse of relentless hardware-related puns about such things as needles opening their eyes in surprise and the nails going on their heads.

I come from a family in which puns were revered, not sneered at. I once watched a fellow approach my brother at a party and say, "Do you have a light?" Whereupon Billy, without a second's hesitation, took a small lamp and held it toward the fellow's cigarette. My mother did a needlepoint for my uncle's antique store that read, "Please Don't Hondle The Merchandise."

"Hondle" is a derogatory term for "negotiate."

Puns are not synonymous with wordplay. If one uses the term "Carmaggedon" to describe the temporary closing of the 405 Freeway in California, the term may be clever and even striking, but it doesn't bust forward with the sweet tang of a well-constructed pun that serves up a familiar word, name, or phrase in a tangy, surprising riff on the word or phrase's understood meaning.

A pun implies a surprise in which you see a concept in a sly new way.

Woody Allen's brand of pun is exemplified by his low-key-yet-audacious remark that "The last time I was in a woman I was visiting the Statue of Liberty."

Some of Woody's writing style, especially in his essays, is a loving nod to S. J. Perelman, who provided the Marx Brothers with some of their best puns in the 1930s. But it wasn't just the humor or the lilt of the language that made Marx Brothers puns so enduring. They spoke to their times. As Roger Ebert put it, they "were the instrument that translated what was once essentially a Jewish style of humor into the dominant note of American comedy. Although they were not taken as seriously, they were as surrealist as Dalí, as shocking as Stravinsky, as verbally outrageous as Gertrude Stein, as alienated as Kafka."

There are t-shirt, poster, and business paraphernalia companies that are known for catering to pun lovers. One t-shirt shows a family having dinner, and the mother quips "All we are saying is give peas a chance." Pick out a birthday card for a friend, and you'll see a range of Gary Larson's "From the Far Side" humor that glorifies the pun at its best and worst ("Finally the animals saw their prey: two baskin robbins.") When it comes to greeting cards, puns have become their Hallmark.

Puns may be, as the English dramatist John Dennis supposedly mused, "the lowest form of humor," but if that is the case, then as his pun-loving contemporary Henry

Erskine punningly countered, that would make them "the foundation of all wit."

Let others prattle on about America's need for greater emphasis on science and math. In my not-so-humble opinion, we need more people who greet puns with a twinkle in their eye, a suppleness in their mind, and a sense of humor lodged firmly in the heart.

—**Gary Blake**
Great Neck, NY
September 2011

Of puns it has been said that those who most
dislike them are those who are
least able to utter them.

CHAPTER 1

Oldies but Goodies

If the ex-president George W. played baseball, would he still be in the bush leagues?

~♦~

The issue of legalizing marijuana will be voted on by a joint session of Congress.

~♦~

There was a tryout party for the Christmas play at the all-girls high school, and every student had the opportunity to eat, drink, and be Mary.

~♦~

When Lizzie Borden made peace with her family, did she bury the hatchet?

~♦~

Two Eskimos sitting in a kayak were chilly, but when they lit a fire in the craft, it sank, proving once again that you can't have your kayak and heat it too.

~♦~

Did you hear about the Buddhist who refused Novocain during a root canal? He wanted to transcend dental medication.

~♦~

A group of chess enthusiasts checked into a hotel and were standing in the lobby discussing their recent tournament victories. After about an hour, the manager came out of the office and asked them to disperse.

"But why?" they asked as they moved.

"Because," he said, "I can't stand chess nuts boasting in an open foyer."

~◆~

A woman has twins and gives them up for adoption. One of them goes to a family in Egypt and is named "Ahmal." The other goes to a family in Spain; they name him "Juan." Years later, Juan sends a picture of himself to his birth mother. Upon receiving the picture, she tells her husband that she wishes she also had a picture of Ahmal. Her husband responds, "They're twins! If you've seen Juan, you've seen Ahmal."

~◆~

What happened when the cow tried to jump over a barbed wire fence? Udder destruction.

~+~

There was a philosophy teacher who no longer wanted to teach in the red-light district because he got tired of putting Descartes before the whores.

~+~

Does the name "Pavlov" ring a bell?

~+~

Mahatma Gandhi, as you know, walked barefoot most of the time, which produced an impressive set of calluses on his feet. He also ate very little, which made him rather frail, and with his odd diet, he suffered from bad breath. This made him . . . what? A super-callused fragile mystic hexed by halitosis.

~+~

There were two ships. One had red paint, one had blue paint. They collided. At last report, the survivors were marooned.

~♦~

A bachelor is a guy who is footloose and fiancée-free.

~♦~

A fellow once sat up all night wondering where the sunshine comes from. . . . Finally, it dawned on him.

~♦~

Alimony is the high cost of leaving.

~♦~

Those who jump off a Paris bridge are in Seine.

~♦~

A bicycle can't stand on its own because it is two tired.

~+~

Acupuncture is a jab well done.

~+~

Seven days without a pun makes one weak.

~+~

There was a man who loved to make up puns. One day, a local magazine sponsored a pun contest. The man entered the contest ten different times in the hope that at least one of his puns would win.

Unfortunately, no pun in ten did.

~+~

In a certain city in eastern Spain, the builder of a movie theater only built a single emergency exit door rather than the two required by law. Sure enough, there was a fire and several people were trampled to death. The moral: Don't put all your Basques in one exit.

~+~

The man who fell into an upholstery machine is fully recovered.

~+~

What's the definition of a will? (It's a dead giveaway.)

~+~

Did you hear about the guy whose whole left side was cut off? He's all right now.

~✦~

A dead writer of music is decomposing.

~✦~

Little Boy to Mother: Today we learned God's name in Sunday school.

Mother: What is it?

Little Boy: It's Harold.

Mother: Harold?

Little Boy: Yes, we sang a hymn: "Praise be to God, Harold be thy name."

~✦~

The Mexican went to the baseball game and sat in the bleachers. He was far away from the field but was touched when everyone in the stadium rose and asked, "José, can you see?"

~✦~

What's a Grecian urn?
Depends on what he does.

~+~

Tailor: Euripides?
Customer: Yes. Eumenides?

~+~

Why did the Indian chief pay for country club membership for his sons?

He wanted to see his red sons in the sail set.

~+~

I thought I saw an eye doctor on an Alaskan island, but it turned out to be an optical Aleutian.

~+~

Two hats were hanging on a hat rack in the hallway. One hat said to the other: "You stay here; I'll go on a head."

~+~

Why does the Pope travel so much? Because he's a roamin' Catholic.

~+~

The blonde had named her dogs Rolex and Timex because they were watch dogs.

~+~

Business at the candle factory tapered off after the holidays.

~+~

On a divorce lawyer's wall: "Satisfaction guaranteed or your honey back."

~+~

The older brother put Krazy Glue on his younger brother's mouth as he slept. Then he warned his brother not to rat on him, but the brother's lips were sealed.

~✦~

She was only a whiskey maker, but he loved her still.

~✦~

A rubber-band pistol was confiscated from algebra class because it was a weapon of math disruption.

~✦~

No matter how much you push the envelope, it'll still be stationery.

~✦~

A grenade thrown into a kitchen in France would result in Linoleum Blownapart.

~✦~

A hole has been found in the nudist camp wall. The police are looking into it.

~♦~

Shotgun wedding: a case of wife or death.

~♦~

In *Star Wars*, Chewbacca was raised on Earth by human parents. He was an excellent athlete and played baseball for the Los Angeles Dodgers. His first year in the big leagues he batted .300 and was named Wookie of the Year.

~♦~

There are three kinds of people. Those that can count and those that can't.

~♦~

The story is told of an African chieftain who lived in a simple grass hut and sat on an elegant, hand carved, wood throne. After ruling for a few years, he decided that wood wasn't good enough for him; he wanted a gold throne. So he commissioned his craftsmen to create a beautiful gold throne, and he took the wood one and stored it in the small attic of his hut.

A few months later, the sounds of warring natives from another tribe were heard approaching the village, and the African chief quickly assumed that they were probably going to steal his gold throne. So he exchanged the thrones, bringing the wooden one back down and hiding the gold throne. While he sat there anticipating the arrival of the enemy tribal warriors, suddenly the gold throne upstairs broke through the ceiling and came crashing down on the chief's head and killed him. So what is the moral of this story? "People in grass houses shouldn't stow thrones."

~✦~

"Ben Battle was a soldier bold and used to war's alarms:
But a cannonball took off his legs, so he laid down his arms."
—Thomas Hood

My wife is a sex object. Every time I ask for sex
. . . she objects.

CHAPTER 2

Sex and the Witty

When a City University of New York doctoral candidate passes his Latin and Greek exams, does that make him a CUNY linguist?

~✦~

When Attila's wife didn't feel like group sex, she told Attila to keep his Huns to himself.

~✦~

If John Holmes were ever tried in court—would he have a hung jury?

~♦~

A man needs a mistress just to break the monogamy.

~♦~

Did you hear about the geologist with an erection? He was between a rock and a hard place.

~♦~

Viagra remains the most popular pill of its kind, despite stiff competition.

~♦~

The first half of the book, which told of his cross-dressing, dragged a bit.

~♦~

You know about the woman who left her massage therapist because he rubbed her the wrong way?

~✦~

Dancing cheek-to-cheek is really a form of floor play.

~✦~

There's a woman whose health insurance picked up the tab for a white noise machine to block out the noise from the bordello across the street; it was considered hormone replacement therapy.

~✦~

When a prostitute loses her job, does she get laid off?

~✦~

His mistress couldn't figure out how to use his desktop computer, but she had no trouble using his laptop.

~✦~

Condoms should be used on every conceivable occasion.

~✦~

I asked him if he was heterosexual, but I couldn't get a straight answer out of him.

~✦~

When they bought a water bed, the couple started to drift apart.

~✦~

Ironically, Dominique Strauss-Kahn wasn't horny at the hotel or with the maid or in court—but he did get off with a small fine.

~✦~

Her clitoral orgasm measured a 7.9 on the Lichter Scale.

~✦~

How do French women hold their liquor? By the ears.

~♦~

I saw a construction truck with the sign on the side: "Well Hung: Windows and Doors."

~♦~

They had used doors in their sex play before but this time they found themselves in a jamb.

~♦~

I knew a woman who resolved to live in a closet until she was ready to admit she was a lesbian. Eventually, she came out.

~♦~

The stripper took off her shoes when she got into her airplane seat. But she started taking off other clothes as the plane started down the runway.

~♦~

Although pursued by many women, he only wanted to sleep with model and actress Campbell. When she rejected him, he thought: "Better laid than Neve."

~♦~

In the privacy of his bedroom, he put his fingers into the liquid remaining after some milk had been curdled and strained. Later, he admitted that it was wonderful: He had never felt this whey before.

~♦~

Oedipus' mom was diagnosed with Porkin' sons.

~♦~

Though a nice guy, he steered away from intercourse and his girlfriends confirmed that, in this area, he never gave an inch.

~+~

She started to throw him out but, within seconds, started ripping his clothes off. He didn't know whether he was coming or going.

~+~

She said she would perform oral sex on him, but he knew she was only paying the idea lip service.

~+~

The only way he could figure out how many women he had oral sex with was to do a head count.

~+~

As diet programs caught on, the shoemaker never got to lose his oral sex virginity because women no longer wanted to eat cobbler.

~♦~

Many women feel that by looking at how large a man's hands are, they can size him up.

~♦~

The man had rubbed his body all over the Venus de Milo before the police came and arrested him for statutory rape.

~♦~

She was a Finnish prostitute who swam every day. She lived up North because she could take a dip and do Laps.

~♦~

After our argument, she put on mascara and lipstick, and we had make-up sex.

~♦~

When Arnold Schwarzenegger started to sleep with his housekeeper, some felt it wasn't about the sex but was merely a cry for help.

~♦~

Every time he started to make love to her, he'd get a charley horse, which really cramped his style.

~♦~

I felt like I would have an orgasm on the interstate, so I took an exit and got off on the exit ramp.

~♦~

Feminine hygiene jokes are the lowest form of humor. Period.

~+~

Which saint had no problem seducing women?
Francis of Asseasy.

~+~

Bond is in bed on top of Dr. Christmas Jones, a brilliant nuclear scientist convincingly portrayed by Denise Richards, who, like all brilliant female nuclear scientists, looks like a supermodel and dresses like Lara Croft. Then James says, "I thought Christmas only comes *once a year*."

~+~

His wife asked him to get two seats to the musical *Man of La Mancha*. Instead, he mistakenly bought two tickets for a sex show called *Woman of La Mancha*. He realized his mistake soon after the orchestra started playing "The Impossible Wet Dream."

~+~

Women should be obscene and not heard.

—Groucho Marx

~✢~

Impotence: nature's way of saying . . . "No hard feelings."

~✢~

There are three stages in a man's life: Tri-Weekly, Try Weekly, and Try Weakly.

~✢~

Having sex is like playing bridge—if you don't have a good partner, you better have a good hand.

❧

I did a theatrical performance about puns.
Really, it was just a play on words.

CHAPTER 3

That's Entertainment

When Edward Albee told his mother he wanted to write *The American Dream*, her reaction was, "Don't be absurd!"

~✦~

When Andy Warhol told his mother he wanted to be an artist, her reaction was "Can it!"

~✦~

When Vincent acted up, Paul would say, "Here we Gauguin."

~♦~

When Georges Seurat told his mother he wanted to be an artist, she said, "What's the point?"

~♦~

Claude Monet never told his mother he wanted to be an artist because he was an impressionable kid.

~♦~

There's one Indian film that has a caste of thousands.

~♦~

When an eel bites your thigh,
And it stings like you'll die,
That's a Moray!

~♦~

Drama critic Percy Hammond couldn't wait for the Fall Season so that he could stone the first cast.

~+~

Sign on a music store window: "Come in and pick out a drum—then beat it!"

~+~

If you break a metal strut on your guitar fingerboard, don't fret.

~+~

Why hear Bono explain that he was not responsible for *Spiderman*'s failure? I refuse to come along and listen to the alibi of Broadway.

~+~

The egotist's favorite song? "Mimi."

~+~

Everyone got plastered for the Beethoven rehearsal. It was the bottom of the Ninth, chorus tight, basses loaded.

~♦~

In one episode of TV's *Frasier*, Daphne is putting on weight and falls down, prompting Frasier, Niles, and Martin all to help her up. Martin, laughing at his own wit, says, "Daphne, I just realized! It took three *Cranes* to lift you!"

~♦~

John and Lorraine had been dating each other for years and were getting bored of each other. They became like a married couple, nagging and sarcastic in all their conversations. One day, John met a girl named Cleary. She was pretty, smart, and funny, and John longed to break up with Lorraine and date Cleary but he couldn't. Then one day Lorraine was walking along the side of a river when she fell in and drowned. When John heard the news he was so happy he sang, "I can see Cleary now; Lorraine has gone."

~♦~

Tina cried when I went away and so did her sister, Marge, but I told them: "Don't cry for me, Marge and Tina."

~+~

Question: What's an Australian kiss?

Answer: The same thing as a French kiss, only down under.

~+~

Even though he was sick with food poisoning, Jerry Seinfeld wanted the nurses to know that he was still Master of his ptomaine.

~+~

I dared an actor to try out for the Blue Man Group—but he was yellow.

~+~

Even the poorest peasant would go to the Winter Palace in St. Petersburg in the evening to see who was dancing with the Tsars.

~•~

There were five or six great actors in *The King's Speech*, but I always think of Colin Firth.

~•~

The thief confronted former *Who Wants to Be a Millionaire* host Regis Philbin and asked, "Do you want me to shoot you?"

Philbin answered, "No, I don't."

The thief asked, "Final answer?"

~•~

I was a theatre major at the University of Wisconsin, but I never acted in a play. Once, however, my foot was in a cast.

~•~

When Hugh Hefner fell in love with a twenty-four-year-old blonde, he thought the marriage would be like a show that lasts forever, but it turned out to be a limited engagement.

~♦~

I saw a subliminal advertising executive, but only for a second.

—Steve Wright

~♦~

When Sting's manager saw him take a fall the day before his sold-out concert, he knew he'd need a hip replacement.

~♦~

Lyricist Oscar Hammerstein to composer Richard Rodger upon meeting at a party: "Who's watching the score?"

~♦~

The comedy about the frozen Persian was quite farsicle.

~♦~

I used to enjoy kabuki theatre, but now I prefer noh drama at all.

~♦~

I set fire to a TV show host and was charged with Arsenio.

~♦~

The Godfather's Sonny Corleone rushed to visit his abused sister in Manhattan but paid a heavy toll.

~♦~

Regarding the *Jack and the Beanstalk* story: "The ends justify the beans."

—Stephen Sondheim

~+~

Imagine Madonna's surprise when she awoke one morning and found that the music business had gone Gaga.

৩৩৩

Pun: "A form of wit, to which wise men stoop and fools aspire."

—Ambrose Bierce

CHAPTER 4

Rich and Infamous

"Do you know the name of the early TV comic who spoke twenty-six languages?"

—Milton Berlitz

~✦~

Does Bernie Madoff have a cell phone?

~✦~

I took Colin Powell to Walter Reade Hospital because he needed an upper GI series, but the surgeon amputated his legs by accident; now, he's a semi-colon.

~+~

Mr. Bellow, the Nobel Prize-winning American author, never varied more than five pounds in his weight during his whole adult life. It was often said that "one size fits Saul."

~+~

If I read about Wonder Woman all day, does that make me a heroine addict?

~+~

What did Phillip II of Macedon say when his son refused to give up the cheese slicer to the maid?

"Alex, hand her the grate."

~+~

The tenth-century Vikings who conquered England also invented advertising and spread word of their conquests using the Norman mailer.

~+~

If Madonna testified in a trial, would she be a material witness?

~+~

If you embezzle money from a rock star, are you involved in a Sting operation?

~+~

In an episode of *Happy Days*, Henry Winkler becomes a financial consultant but insists he is not running a Fonzi scheme.

~+~

At Jenny Craig's, lazy workers are "downsized."

~♦~

Winona Ryder has a hernia and her agent doesn't want her lifting anything anymore.

~♦~

As George Brett said when asked about his hemorrhoids, "That's all behind me."

~♦~

Bernie Madoff: He lived large, was caught, and went to prison. That's the way the crook-he crumbled.

~♦~

Princess Diana and other British yuppies who lived along Sloan Square and King's Road were known as Sloan Rangers.

~♦~

International Monetary Fund head Dominique Strauss-Kahn, who was yanked off a jet and arrested in the alleged sodomy attack of a hotel housekeeper, has told reporters the name of the song he whistles when in court. It's "You Maid—Me Love You (I Didn't Want to Do It; I Didn't Want To Do It)."

~✦~

The Libyan leader was so fond of marshmallows and chocolate that behind his back he was called Mallomar Ghadafi.

~✦~

I asked a friend in Georgia if he wanted to go on a safari with me, but he said he had already seen vast stretches of Savannah.

~✦~

The two Wong brothers went to Beijing's Tiananmen Square to march for the right to assemble, but they were arrested. Two Wongs didn't make a right.

~✦~

King Charles I struggled with Parliament because they handled him in a Cavalier manner.

~✦~

Steig Larsson told me he had a novel way to use the same characters in each of his books.

~✦~

The rebels had won the war and broken into Saddam's home. When they opened his refrigerator, all they saw were open mayonnaise bottles, month-old coleslaw, rotting lemons, and other foods way past their expiration dates: These were the spoils of war.

~✦~

A filibuster is a Capitol offense.

~+~

Although the anchors of the three major networks all rented cars at San Francisco International Airport, Wolf Blitzer got stuck taking a cable car.

~+~

Salvador Dalí drew hundreds of drawings toward the end of his life because he needed the money—his account was overdrawn.

~+~

Prince Charles, if he assumes the throne, might not elevate Camilla's position—but he wouldn't rule it out.

~♦~

When Sarah Palin was asked her thoughts on syntax, she said that she was not in favor of either.

~♦~

Was there a less violent option for Macbeth killing the king? Yes, he could have put poison in Duncan's donuts.

~♦~

When Yoko was down on her luck, her proctologist worked probe Ono.

~♦~

It's not important that you once smoked marijuana; it's important that you quit while you were a head.

~♦~

A director is screen testing Sylvester Stallone and Arnold Schwarzenegger for a new film about classic composers. Not having figured out whom to give which part he asks Sly who he would like to be. Stallone says, "I like Mozart. I want to be Mozart!" So, the director says, "Very well, you can be Mozart." Then he turns to Arnie and says, "Arnie, who would you like to play?"

And Arnie says, "Ah'll be Bach!"

~♦~

If you think guests really enjoy your home movies, you are probably projecting.

~♦~

The second-richest man in the world hates restaurants and has even declared a war on buffets.

~♦~

He thought he could trade funny remarks with Oscar Wilde, but he just wasn't equipped.

~♦~

Davy Crockett had three ears. A left ear, a right ear, and a wild frontier.

~♦~

To this day, all Ford air conditioners display their names: "Norm, Hi & Max." The three Goldberg brothers, Norman, Hyman, and Maxwell, invented and developed the first automobile air conditioner. They went to Henry Ford and told him they had developed the most exciting innovation in the auto industry since the invention of the electric starter.

Ford asked them what it was, and they responded by taking him outside to their car. It was a hot day, temperatures in the high 90s. They got into the car, which was 130 degrees inside, and turned on the air conditioner. The car cooled down immediately.

Ford was very excited and offered them $3 million for the patent. The brothers refused the offer, saying they would settle for $2 million, but they demanded recognition by having a label "The Goldberg Air-Conditioner" installed on the dashboard of every car with an air conditioner. Ford was anti-Semitic and was not about to put the Goldberg name on millions of his cars. They haggled for several hours and finally agreed on $3 million, but only the first name of each Goldberg brother would be displayed.

~✦~

Groucho: All along the river, those are all levees.
Chico: That's the Jewish neighborhood?

—from *The Cocoanuts*

"A pun is a short quip followed by a long groan."
—Author unknown

CHAPTER 5

Newsworthy Notables

I was asked who invented the guillotine but didn't know off the top of my head.

~✦~

When Freud told his mother he wanted to be a world-renowned psychotherapist, she said, "Keep dreaming!"

~✦~

If the al-Qaeda living in Afghanistan are psychotic, and the al-Qaeda living in Pakistan are neurotic, does that make the al-Qaeda living between these countries borderline personalities?

~♦~

The late Queen Mother, addressing her two servants, asked, "Will one of you two old queens get this old queen a drink?"

~♦~

Adlai Stevenson, once asked to comment on Pope Paul and Norman Vincent Peale, said: "I find Paul appealing and Peale appalling."

~♦~

King Ozymandias of Assyria was running low on cash after years of war with the Hittites. His last great possession was the Star of the Euphrates, the most valuable diamond in the ancient world. Desperate, he went to Croesus, the pawnbroker, to ask for a loan. Croesus said, "I'll give you 100,000 dinars for it." "But I paid a million dinars for it," the king protested. "Don't you know who I am? I am the king!" Croesus replied, "When you wish to pawn a star, makes no difference who you are."

~✦~

When I asked Pavarotti if he'd be kind enough to sing a song from *The Music Man*, I knew I was asking for "Trouble."

~✦~

Churchill received the following telegram from Shaw: "Here are two tickets to my play. Bring a friend—if you have one."

Churchill wired back to Shaw: "Cannot come to the opening night. But will be happy to attend the second night—if you have one."

This was a Churchillian example of a barbed wire.

~+~

The weekday Christian radio show hosted by failed apocalypse predictor Harold Camping was taken off the air. His wife comforted him by saying, "Look, Harold, it's not the end of the world."

~+~

I. M. Pei argued that not all of Frank Lloyd Wright's buildings were made of wood or stone, but he couldn't come up with a single concrete example.

~+~

George W. Bush once owned an oil company—but he drove it into the ground.

~♦~

Whenever I get the insatiable need to see a TV news magazine show immediately, my friend will advise me to wait 60 minutes.

~♦~

I was open to trying LSD in the 1960s, but many of my friends were a bit Leary.

~♦~

To fix a parking ticket in the capital city of Texas, you have to be on good terms with the Austin Powers that be.

~♦~

Only old women watch the Grammy Awards.

~♦~

Occasionally, the Pope has private meetings with heads of state, even those who are imprisoned. Mubarak of Egypt was part of a captive audience.

~✦~

When I am dead
I hope it may be said
His sins were scarlet
But his books were read.

—Hillaire Belloc

~✦~

"You can lead a horticulture, but you can't make her think."

—Dorothy Parker

~✦~

Charlie Sheen bought a bikini made out of money for his new girlfriend because he likes to watch his Green Goddess dressing.

~✦~

According to one tenth-grade textbook, after Luther nailed his ninety-five theses to a church door, he was punished by being made to exist on a Diet of Worms.

~♦~

"So, Robin Hood, roughly how long have you been in your current occupation?" He replied, "A few years. Give or take."

~♦~

Unfortunately for the Cisco Kid, it was pouring rain and he couldn't remember where he last saw his pancho.

~♦~

He was trying to replace the town plumber, who had been there for thirty years, and had become a regular fixture.

~♦~

It was Noel Coward who uttered the oft-quoted line, "Keir Dullea, Gone Tomorrow."

~•~

I was visiting France, and, while in Paris, I decided to take a guided tour around the beautiful cathedral on the banks of the Seine. As we were being shown around the building, all of a sudden I spotted a sandwich box lying on the floor.

So I picked it up and handed it to the guide. He was very apologetic and hurried off with it. After a few minutes, I could hear him calling up the bell tower: "Quasimodo! You left your sandwich box lying around again!"

When the guide returned, he apologized again, and when we asked him about the sandwiches, he said: "Don't worry about it . . . it's just the lunch pack of Notre Dame."

~•~

William Penn, the founder and mayor of Philadelphia, had two aunts—Hattie and Sophia—who were skilled in the baking arts. One day, "Big Bill" was petitioned by the citizens of his town because the three bakeries in the town had, during the Revolution, raised the price of pies to the point that only the rich could afford them. Not wanting to challenge the bakeries directly, he turned to his aunts and asked their advice. But when they had heard the story, the two old ladies were so incensed over the situation that they offered to bake one hundred pies themselves and sell them for two cents less that any of the bakeries were charging. It was a roaring success. Their pies sold out quickly, and very soon they had managed to bring down the price of all kinds of pastry in Philadelphia. That's how Gilbert and Sullivan were inspired to write The Pie Rates of Penn's Aunts.

~✦~

Shortly after the Korean War, the son of then South Korean President Syngman Rhee was hired as a *Life Magazine* correspondent. The younger Rhee was a remarkably kind, gentle, and considerate man, but he had one problem: He loved to drink and could be gone on a bender for days.

On one occasion, Rhee was missing for three days before someone at the magazine's office finally suggested they look for him. Other correspondents, and even the police, were involved in the search.

Finally, about two weeks later, a policeman walked into a tavern, looked at the man slumped over the bar and cried, "Ah, Sweet Mr. Rhee of Life, at last I've found you."

~✦~

Mae West once said that she once was pure as the driven snow, but then she drifted.

~♦~

Charles Dickens was despondent in a Paris bar, telling the bartender, "It is the worst of times, for I am without an idea for a new work. Let me partake of a vodka martini," to which the bartender responded, "Olive or twist?"

~♦~

Dr. Samuel Johnson's coming up with the idea of writing a dictionary was the defining moment of his life.

~♦~

Usually, having a flop TV show hurts your career. Yet, Ted Danson has survived a flop and still has his pick of new TV roles. It just goes to prove that "Beckers can be choosers."

~＊~

After Quasimodo was killed, the guy hired to replace him turned out to be a dead ringer for him.

~＊~

Paul Revere hated all horses, and on his midnight ride, he chose a horse that was a real nightmare.

~＊~

Narcissistic and beautiful, Paris Hilton is often referred to as "I-candy."

~＊~

Evidence has been found that William Tell and his family were avid bowlers. Unfortunately, all the Swiss league records were destroyed in a fire. Thus we'll never know for whom the Tells bowled.

CRYP

"A good pun is its own reword."

—Author unknown

CHAPTER 6

Brand Hex

There's a new cereal for people in a hurry: Post Haste.

~✦~

When it comes to headache pain, I can take it or Aleve it.

~✦~

Most people who make felt tip pens have a flair for it.

~✦~

Is the Pillsbury Dough Boy a flour child?

~✦~

The bookie had no money so he paid in grape juice, which was the first time he ever Welched on a bet.

~✦~

The Marquis de Sade's favorite dessert: Whip N' Chill.

~♦~

I spent days trying to fix my GPS but was getting nowhere fast.

~♦~

He had gotten food poisoning from Greek cheese in the past, but this time he complained it was a Feta worse than death.

~♦~

The nude bathers didn't mind that the police asked them to put on their bathing suits, but they did object to the Coppertone.

~•~

The electrician went to Vienna, where he ate his first socket torte, which provided him with a much-needed outlet.

~•~

I've tried ordering Doan's Pills—but they're always on back-order.

~•~

Since I won't pay full price for a diamond, let me know when it goes on Zale.

~•~

The CEO of the Wurlitzer Company has decided to leave his organs to science.

~♦~

There's great new stain remover for idiots; it's called "Oxymoron."

~♦~

The shipmates grumbled because everyone from the first mate to the purser forgot to buy paper towels for the dishes, leading to a mutiny on the Bounty.

~♦~

The children didn't mind the fact that the woman selling Good Humor in the neighborhood was pushing seventy, but the parents knew she had been around the block a few times.

~♦~

Whenever I feel myself losing energy, I just put a Slinky in my shoe and that adds a spring to my step.

~+~

I ran into a box of Kleenex last night and suffered some soft tissue injuries.

~+~

The shampoo cost very little, but it was head and shoulders above the others.

~+~

When she reached her goal weight, she still bought her food from Jenny Craig because it tasted good and she figured she had nothing to lose.

~+~

He had five thousand shares of Coca-Cola but had almost no liquid assets.

~♦~

An Irishman named O'Malley proposed to his girl on St. Patrick's Day . . . he gave her a ring with a synthetic diamond.

The excited young lass showed it to her father, a jeweler. He took one look at it and saw it was not real.

The young lass, on learning it wasn't real, returned to her future husband. She protested vehemently about his cheapness. "In honor of St. Patrick's Day," he said while smiling, "I gave you a sham rock."

❧

When a ladder was stolen from a store, the manager said that further steps would be taken.

CHAPTER 7

It's a Living

I wanted to be a stenographer, but the HR manager said that the company is not short-handed at the moment.

~✦~

When an electrician is terminal, do the doctors pull the plug on him?

~✦~

My landscaper keeps trying to get me to invest in hedge funds.

~♦~

Impatient dermatologists make rash judgments.

~♦~

I used to work in the Chinese export business, but then I got jaded.

~♦~

He became a partner during his third year at college—a junior partner.

~♦~

I used to want to be a Skycap, but now I know it's not my bag.

~♦~

A butcher backed into a meat grinder and got a little behind in his work.

~♦~

The name of Tonto's son, who works at FedEx, is Pronto.

~♦~

If a stringer of pearls is abandoned by his colleagues, is he stranded?

~♦~

One golfer got his pilot's license and was always flying off-course.

~♦~

A psychic successfully marketed her service through the Seer's Catalog.

~♦~

As I said to my copyeditor, "Mark my words . . ."

~♦~

Do retired handymen live on a fixed income?

~♦~

When elevator operators are fired, they are shown the door.

~♦~

When firefighters lose their jobs, are they fired or given the axe?

~+~

Are farmers who lose their jobs put out to pasture?

~+~

A new chain of opticians is called Site for Sore Eyes.

~+~

I used to work at Starbucks, but I got tired of the daily grind.

~+~

I used to work in a blanket factory, but the company folded.

~+~

I bet the butcher the other day that he couldn't reach the meat that was on the top shelf. He refused to take the bet, saying that the steaks were too high.

~•~

Did you hear about the optometrist who fell into a lens grinder and made a spectacle of himself?

~•~

Santa's helpers are subordinate Clauses.

~•~

The short fortune-teller who escaped from prison was a small medium at large.

~•~

The gladiator was having a rough day in the arena. His opponent had sliced off both of his arms. Nevertheless, he kept on fighting, kicking, and biting as furiously as he could. But when his opponent lopped off both feet, our gladiator had no choice but to give up, for now he was both unarmed and defeated.

~+~

A prisoner's favorite punctuation mark is the period. It marks the end of his sentence.

~+~

The guy who invented the doorknocker got a No-bell Prize.

~+~

A baker stopped making donuts after he got tired of the hole thing.

~+~

Some burglars are always looking for windows of opportunity.

~+~

A scientist doing a large experiment with liquid chemicals was trying to solve a problem when he fell in and became part of the solution.

~+~

A woman who only dated roofers and firemen who climbed ladders was looking for love in all the rung places.

~+~

When the glassblower inhaled, he got a pane in the stomach.

~+~

I knew a mathematician who didn't believe in negative numbers—and would stop at nothing to prove it.

~♦~

I stopped dating the librarian because she was always reading things into everything I said.

~♦~

Another librarian I knew ran a side business off the books.

~♦~

A former Rockette doesn't like to talk about her work because it kicks up too many sad memories for her.

~♦~

Jackhammer operators like to break new ground.

~♦~

I do a lot of spreadsheets in the office, so you might say I'm excelling at work.

~♦~

The telegraph operator who accidentally sent the same message twice was remorseful.

~♦~

The tea industry is in hot water, but the kettle industry is going full steam ahead!

~♦~

He knew he'd run out of spray paint before he was finished because he could see the handwriting on the wall.

~♦~

Do you know about the electrician who drank so much coffee he was completely wired?

~♦~

I knew a biased court illustrator who was always drawing his own conclusions.

~ + ~

That morning, the writer interviewed for a job writing collection letters to debtors, and, before he knew it, it was a dun deal.

~ + ~

They had dreams of having a world famous architect design their house but could only do it on a Pei-as-you-go-basis.

~ + ~

Pastry chefs know that old age crepes up on you.

~ + ~

My dental hygienist seemed distracted. I think she was brushing me off.

~•~

Old printers never die; they just revert to type.

~•~

I used to be a fisherman, but I got caught playing hooky.

~•~

I used to be a banker but lost interest in the work.

~•~

The seamstress's business was off 60 percent, and if you asked her how she was doing, she'd say, "Just so-so."

~•~

The carpenter with a childhood habit was still biting his nails.

~✦~

The orthodontist wrote a book, a do-it-yourself orthodonture called *Brace Yourself!*

~✦~

In Southern California and Southern Florida, psychics read only palms.

~✦~

Do Arctic sommeliers worry about the wine-chill factor?

~✦~

He was a skilled carpenter whose untalented partner was his brother-in-law, so he couldn't really level with him.

~✦~

The stagecoach driver was fired after a binge and was not rehired, even when he promised to go on the wagon.

~♦~

Since the kitchen was small, the contractor felt that building a granite island would be counter-productive.

~♦~

When the two greatest bowlers of their generation began their match, the audience was silent. In fact, you could hear a pin drop.

~♦~

I asked my friend what it was like to work in the cutlery industry, and he told me, "There's never a dull moment."

~♦~

Debbie, part of a renowned fireworks family, studied with fireworks masters but still had to take a test to become certified in her field. As predicted, she passed with flying colors.

~✦~

The father in Nepal said to his son, "Do you want to learn how to guide people up Mount Everest?" His son said, "Sure, Pa."

~✦~

Like tavern owners, ballet dancers make most of their money at the barre.

~✦~

A Filipino man was hired by the circus as a contortionist—he was the first Manila folder.

~✦~

The first accountant to be hired by a circus was caught juggling the books.

~✦~

My Aunt Lyla asked me if I wanted an apple pie, a blueberry pie, or a pecan pie. I told her to decide, but she said she couldn't. "Why not?" I asked.

"Because," said Lyla, "Bakers can't be choosers."

~✦~

"Attention staff! The clothes keep falling off the mannequins in ladies' wear. Would someone please redress the problem?"

~✦~

The police said to the bootlegger: "You can rum , but you can't hide!"

~✦~

The electrician and the air hostess got on really well together. Sparks flew!

~+~

The dentist put braces on his patient as a stop-gap measure.

~+~

The sign at a gynecologist's office: "Dr. Jones, at your cervix."

~+~

"They laughed when I said I was going to be a comedian. They're not laughing now."

—Bob Monkhouse, comedian (1928–2003)

~+~

The chiropractor received a tax deduction for his second computer because it was a back-up.

~♦~

Soon after Fred received a patent for discovering lower-case letters, Jack applied for a patent for upper-case letters. Fred launched a patent infringement suit against Jack, who he claimed capitalized on his idea.

~♦~

I used to be a ballet dancer but found it too-too difficult.

~♦~

On January 17, 1902, the first gum factory opened. An employee fell into the vat and his boss chewed him out.

~♦~

A dentist and a manicurist married. They fought tooth and nail.

~♦~

I was on an elevator the other day, and the operator kept calling me "son."

I said, "Why do you keep calling me 'son'? You're not my father."

He said, "I brought you up, didn't I?"

~+~

A college president warned the alumni chairman against requesting too much money at one time by saying, "Don't put all your begs in one ask it."

~+~

A lawyer for a church did some cross-examining.

~+~

Undertakers Mal and Mel were storing embalming fluid. It was considered appropriate to place it in an area out of sight.

Mel had his share stored promptly but there was still a good portion left for Mal to take care of. When asked why he had not just stored it all, Mel said, "The rest is for Mal to hide."

~♦~

I called the plumber on the phone: "Can you come over and fix my kitchen sink again?" His encouraging reply: "You know I'm always at your disposal."

~♦~

A dry cleaner was indicted for money laundering. A deal is being ironed out.

~♦~

"A friend of mine has a business measuring the relative sizes of the rises, drops, cavities, and undulations of underwater coral formations."

"Sounds like a good job. Is it steady work?"

"He only works in the summer months. He takes the winters off to avoid the frigid air."

"You mean . . . ?"

"Yes. He's a frost-free reef ridge rater."

෴

At some executive meetings there
is a chairman of the bored.

CHAPTER 8

Languid
Language

A Freudian slip is when you say one thing but mean your mother.

~♦~

A new book on do-it-yourself brain surgery is titled *Suture Self*.

~♦~

I knew that until I agreed with him on his definition of infinity, I would never hear the end of it.

~✦~

My wife really likes to make pottery, but to me it's just kiln time.

~✦~

Did you hear about the fire at the campground The heat was intense.

~✦~

Although she loved having Chinese soup, it gave her wanton desires.

~✦~

I was jailed for stealing after my therapist concluded that my diagnosis was "arrested development."

~✦~

Reading while sunbathing will make you well red.

~+~

I used to go to an origami class . . . until it folded.

~+~

There was a fantasy-prone hooker whose eyes were playing tricks on her.

~+~

He'd buy a pair of pants and then, a month later, have them taken out.

This happened repeatedly: buy, enlarge.

~+~

Would you call him a panhandler? Homeless? Poverty stricken? A bum?

All of these labels beggar the question.

~♦~

For his friend, who enjoyed making hash brownies, he bought a matching set of potholders.

~♦~

Islam is not a synonym for terrorists. It has many humanitarian causes. For example, take the Mecca Wish Foundation.

~♦~

The police called in the owner of a local delicatessen to help translate what a young boy was saying, because, apparently, he was speaking in tongues.

~♦~

I bought a few negative numbers the other day because they were on sale; in fact, they cost next to nothing.

~+~

To his Greek professor's frustration, Jim would recite the Greek alphabet saying, "Alpha, Gamma, Delta, Epsilon . . . " After a while, the professor realized that Jim was taking a Beta blocker.

~+~

I asked the director of the Musee d'Orsay if he liked the work of Warhol and he replied, "Oui. Un soupcon."

~+~

He was tired of smoking grass and scared to try heroin, but he figured that methamphetamines were about his speed.

~+~

When the doctor left the room, the patient immediately picked up the Band-Aid that was on the doctor's desk and put it in his pocket. He had always been told that when ripping a Band-Aid off, you should do it quickly.

~♦~

After she received the epidural, she closed her eyes and said softly, "I'm . . . we've . . . don't . . . wouldn't . . . can't . . . " The husband smiled because the contractions were coming every minute now.

~♦~

Benny was sure that if he had to, he could master Braille once he got a feel for it.

~♦~

When the glacier was asked his opinions on global warming he replied, "I dunno, I've never really thawed about it."

~♦~

Can a boat join the fleet if it's slow?

~+~

I dated a fitness instructor, but we just never seemed to work out.

~+~

If a Republican wins the presidency by promising to cut Obamacare, is that elective surgery?

~+~

He took her to a fancy restaurant on their first date. He said, "Dinner's on me. Have any anything you want as long as it doesn't cost more than $10."

She looked at him and said, "That's no way to treat a lady."

~+~

Instead of a company picnic, every employee had to attend one opera a year.

No one questioned this policy; it was just part of the corporate culture.

~•~

At the end, I wanted to work in a funny pun about Arizona Iced Tea, but the subject was intrinsically without Yuma.

~•~

On the ship's deck, his vital signs were good, but, when he went to his room, he would develop a low-grade cabin fever.

~•~

In France, they make their omelets with only one egg. You see, in France one egg is an oeuf.

~◆~

I know a man whose wife thought she had terminal cancer yet she wouldn't see a doctor. My friend was so frustrated he thought about walking out on her. I advised against it, noting that "The unexamined wife isn't worth leaving."

~◆~

Penny was a hard-working, conscientious girl who lived on her own. Her dream in life was to go on an ocean cruise around the world. So she scrimped, and she saved, and she saved, and she scrimped until finally, one day, she had enough money to go on her ocean cruise. One night, after they had been at sea for a week, Penny was walking back to her cabin when the heel on her left shoe broke, throwing her off balance. The ship chose that moment to tilt to the left. As a result, Penny was thrown overboard. A hue and a cry were immediately raised, and after about five minutes, they found Penny. Hauling her aboard, the ship's crew realized that it was too late. Poor Penny was dead. Normally, they would have done a burial at sea, but, as I said before, Penny was a very conscientious girl and had written a will. In it, she specified that she wished for her body to be cremated and kept in a jar on her parents' fireplace mantel. Her wishes were fulfilled, which just goes to show you that a Penny saved is a Penny urned.

~✦~

Candles were first used on a birthday cake for people who wanted to make light of their age.

~+~

After carelessly plucking her eyebrows while shopping for a corsage, Rose couldn't see the florist because of the tweeze.

~+~

Abstinence leaves a lot to be desired.

~+~

A boy was bagging groceries at a supermarket. One day, the store installed a machine for squeezing fresh orange juice. Intrigued, the young man asked if he could be allowed to work the machine, but his request was denied. Said the store manager, "Sorry, kid, but baggers can't be juicers."

~+~

I used to have a fear of hurdles, but I got over it.

~♦~

The secretary of state was so afraid that the budget for missiles would be cut that it made him sick to his stomach and led to a night of projectile vomiting.

~♦~

Did you hear about the big winner on *Jeopardy!*? He went home the next day, and his wife demanded, "Who were those women I saw you outwit last night?"

~+~

Sign on a broken perfume bottle, "Out of odor."

൜

> "I'm a peripheral visionary."
> —Steven Wright

CHAPTER 9

Odds and Ends

Is an obese person who chooses not to diet going on his gut instinct?

~♦~

Most men who wear three-piece suits have a vested interest in dressing well.

~♦~

The MapQuest software that showed his home town was incomplete because someone left a block off the old chip.

~+~

I called MapQuest to report the problem, but they refused to address it.

~+~

Bugs have very diverse religious views because they are all in sects.

~+~

Do you know about the perennially late bowler who missed a split because he had no time to spare?

~+~

The special room where the ship's captain took notes on the voyage was known as the log cabin.

~+~

I knew a Magic Marker user who was always blacking out.

~+~

He only smoked grass when there was a bull market because he believed in buying low and selling high.

~+~

It will cost you a lot for hospitalization if you drop your cable box on your foot because you'll have to see a doctor out of network.

~+~

If you don't pay your exorcist, you get repossessed.

~+~

A backwards poet writes inverse.

~+~

In a democracy, it's your vote that counts. In a monarchy, it's your count that votes.

~♦~

Does a biker, identified with a product or charity, become its spokesperson?

~♦~

If a man calls balls and strikes at a baseball game in Istanbul, is he an Ottoman Umpire?

~♦~

Is it true that midgets have a poor sense of humor because most jokes go over their heads?

~♦~

When a clock is hungry it goes back for seconds.

~♦~

I was fixated on the pain in my bad tooth. I was abscessed by it

~ ♦ ~

Q. What is one of the first things that Adam and Eve did after they were kicked out?

A. They really raised Cain whenever they were Able.

~ ♦ ~

She has more chins than a Hong Kong phonebook.

~ ♦ ~

You feel stuck with your debt if you can't budge it.

~ ♦ ~

A patient came running to my psychiatry office screaming, "I'm a teepee! I'm a wigwam!" I told him, "Relax, you're two tents."

~ ♦ ~

After working for twenty-four hours straight, he called it a day.

~♦~

Do the people who climb the world's highest mountain ever rest?

~♦~

When there's a sale on tennis balls, it's first come, first serve.

~♦~

His watermelon had seeds because he believed in plant parenthood.

~♦~

Passover—the days of wine and *charoses*.

~ ✦ ~

Bakers trade bread recipes on a knead-to-know basis.

~ ✦ ~

Usually, Donald Trump enjoyed playing Bridge, but today he felt especially vulnerable.

~ ✦ ~

So many lottery winners had gone broke that the lottery became known as a "debt giveaway."

~ ✦ ~

His life combined using his van to transport people's belongings with his religious practice of sitting at prayer and waiting for the spirit to move him, often culminating in a violent reaction. He was a mover and a Shaker.

~+~

The agreeable tennis umpire was generous to a fault.

~+~

Her rhinoplasty was not covered by Medicare, so, unfortunately, she paid through the nose for it.

~+~

Lightning sometimes shocks people because it just doesn't know how to conduct itself.

~+~

How do they refer to Coke, Pepsi, and other sodas in the Midwest?

(Warning: Later you may have a pop quiz.)

~•~

The aging beautician worked until she was ninety-seven and then dyed in her sleep.

~•~

The fact that they would probably spend the rest of their lives in a mental hospital didn't stop them from having a committed relationship.

~•~

It's hard to get ivory in Africa, but in Alabama the Tuscaloosa.

~•~

The Zen enthusiast said to the hot dog vendor: "Make me one with everything."

~♦~

Did you see the movie about the cannibal that consumed his mother-in-law?

It was named *Gladiator.*

~♦~

We're not getting anywhere in geometry class. It feels like we're going in circles.

~♦~

I had trouble getting to the university in New Orleans. I had to drive down a two-lane road.

~♦~

A noun and a verb were dating, but they broke up because the noun was too possessive.

~♦~

The indecisive rower couldn't choose either oar.

~♦~

Once the Gregorian Calendar became accepted, it was clear that the Julian Calendar's days were numbered.

~♦~

I am not drunk—and I feel that is a loaded question.

~♦~

They threw me off the tug of war team because they felt I wasn't pulling my weight.

~♦~

He found that fitting into his new denim was a cinch.

~♦~

Although most warts are caused by viruses, some can come from stress. These, the doctors refer to as "worry warts."

~♦~

When my date shook hands with me, her hands were freezing, which told me she had been out of circulation for a while.

~♦~

She was tired after shopping for her iPhone, so she decided to take an app.

~♦~

In a Water Mill, New York, antique shop, a sign reads: "Please Don't Hondle the Merchandise."

~+~

A man who could barely touch his knees tried to touch his toes, knowing it would be quite a stretch for him.

~+~

The father said: "It would be my fervent hope that you would be slapped."

"Stop," shouted the son, "You're being passive aggressive."

~+~

As an observant Jew, he only ate fast food on Yom Kippur.

~♦~

The administration decided that, for fairness sake, they wouldn't hand out paychecks in alphabetical order of the employee.

This didn't cause rancor among the employees but many were staggered.

~♦~

The owners of the new ball field only created a few hot dog stands and were unprepared when the crowds demanded a variety of snacks. Clearly, concessions had to be made.

~♦~

The Republicans refused to consider any new taxes, yet they labeled the Democrats as having a "Debt Wish."

~♦~

He saw no irony in the fact that he was awarded a master's degree in communication based on his dissertation about "Don't Ask, Don't Tell."

~+~

When the cog met the wheel, it was love at first sight. Before long, they were engaged.

~+~

When I asked the Tea Party member what he didn't like, he said, "The government." I asked what he liked. He said, "No gun control." I asked him what else he was against. He answered, "Taxes."

Clearly, this man was a rebel without a clause.

~+~

Instead of paying the orthodontist each time their son went to see him, his parents decided to keep the orthodontist on retainer.

~+~

The first Chinese mail delivery was made by boat—it delivered only junk mail.

~❖~

Harry wouldn't settle for saying goodbye in the foyer. He kept his "goodbye" going as you walked to your car over the front yard.

It was just too much: I hate lawn "goodbyes."

~❖~

The book of incantations was useless. The author had failed to run a spell check.

~❖~

A man went to his dentist because something felt wrong in his mouth. The dentist examined him and said, "That new upper plate I put in for you six months ago is eroding. What have you been eating?"

The man replied, "All I can think of is that about four months ago my wife made some asparagus and put some stuff on it that was delicious . . . Hollandaise sauce. I loved it so much I now put it on everything—meat, toast, fish, vegetables, everything."

"Well," said the dentist, "that's probably the problem. Hollandaise sauce is made with lots of lemon juice, which is highly corrosive. It's eaten away your upper plate. I'll make you a new plate, and this time use chrome."

"Why chrome?" asked the patient.

To which the dentist replied, "It's simple. Everyone knows that there's no plate like chrome for the Hollandaise!"

~✦~

At Scotland's Glasgow University, the following note was seen hanging on a lecturer's door: "Today's tutorial is canceled because Dr. N. is il." After the misspelled final word, a student had penciled in: "(sic)."

~+~

A practical Czech is considered to be Praguematic.

~+~

When I saw a wicker furniture outlet in Copenhagen, I knew there was something rattan in the state of Denmark.

~+~

There once was a small town in which lived a group of monks. These monks, having need of money to fund their monastery, decided to open a flower shop. Well, the rest of the townspeople were very pleased at first, since they hadn't had a flower shop before. However, some people became concerned when they noticed that whenever children were sent to the flower shop to buy (you guessed it!) flowers, they went missing.

A group of citizens went to the shop to see if the monks knew what had happened to them. They entered the store and were immediately impressed and awed by the wide assortment of exotic flora present. However, their admiration turned to horror when one of the larger plants reached down, grabbed a small boy, and swallowed him whole!

The villagers fled the shop screaming, attracting the attention of the other townspeople. As soon as the news was spread, the people decided that the only thing to do was to get rid of the evil monks.

A group of twenty men armed themselves with clubs and staves. At high noon, they attacked the monks' flower shop. However, they were unprepared for the high level of fighting skills of the brown-robed brothers: The men were beaten back in less than fifteen minutes!

So the townspeople assembled a second group, this time arming them with knives and scythes. At midnight, they attacked. But once again, the merciless monks beat them back, this time in less than ten minutes!

The townspeople were at a loss. Who would save them from the corrupt Capuchins? Suddenly, out of the darkness, stepped Hugh the blacksmith, the tallest, strongest, and most foul-smelling man in the village.

"Do not worry, my friends," said Hugh. "I will rid this town of these evil evangelists!"

The townspeople, having no other alternative, armed Hugh with clubs, staves, knives, and scythes, and sent him off to vanquish the foul friars. They waited impatiently at the edge of the town, hoping against hope that Hugh would return victorious.

Suddenly, over the crest of the hill, silhouetted against the afternoon sun, appeared Hugh. Over his shoulder was slung the remains of the hideous man-eating plant. "The monks have fled! Their flowers will trouble us no more!" cried Hugh. The townspeople cried out with joy, and, proclaiming the day a holiday, feasted and danced until dawn. From that day on, a moral was passed on to all the children of the town. Whenever they were tempted to make fun of Hugh and his slow, smelly ways, they were reminded:

"Only Hugh can prevent florist friars."

❦

" . . . No circumstances, however dismal, will ever be considered a sufficient excuse for the admission of that last and saddest evidence of intellectual poverty, the Pun."
—Mark Twain, *A Biography*

CHAPTER 10

Animal Puns

A three-legged dog walks into a saloon in the Old West. He slides up to the bar and announces: "I'm looking for the man who shot my paw."

~ ✦ ~

Did you hear about the promiscuous queen bee who tested HIVE-positive?

~ ✦ ~

If you throw a cat out a car window, does it become kitty litter?

~✦~

Did the matador kick the bull as the bull ran toward his red cape?

The judge determined that the matador was guilty as charged.

~✦~

Two silk worms had a race. They ended up in a tie.

~✦~

I paid the veterinarian by check when I had my cat neutered, and he marked the bill "Spayed in Full."

~✦~

The best way to stop a charging bull is to take away his credit card.

~✦~

The duck said to the bartender, "Put it on my bill."

~✦~

It's okay to watch elephants bathe as long as they wear their trunks.

~✦~

A chicken crossing the road is poultry in motion.

~ ♦ ~

A horse walks into a bar. The bartender says, "So, why the long face?"

~ ♦ ~

When he suggested making children's cookies in the shape of animals, they thought he was crackers.

~ ♦ ~

As she laid her pet on the table, the vet pulled out his stethoscope and listened to the bird's chest. After a moment or two, the vet shook his head sadly and said, "I'm so sorry, your duck Cuddles has passed away."

The distressed owner wailed, "Are you sure?"

"Yes, I am sure. The duck is dead," he replied.

"How can you be so sure," she protested. "I mean, you haven't done any testing on him or anything. He might just be in a coma or something."

The vet rolled his eyes, turned around, left the room, and returned a few moments later with a black Labrador Retriever. As the duck's owner looked on in amazement, the dog stood on his hind legs, put his front paws on the examination table and sniffed the duck from top to bottom. He then looked at the vet with sad eyes and shook his head. The vet patted the dog, took it out, and returned a few moments later with a cat.

The cat jumped up on the table and also sniffed delicately at the bird from head to foot. The cat sat back on its haunches, shook its head, meowed softly, and strolled out of the room.

The vet looked at the woman and said, "I'm sorry, but as I said, this is most definitely, 100-percent-certifiably, a dead duck." Then the vet turned to his computer terminal, hit a few keys, and produced a bill, which he handed to the woman. The duck's owner, still in shock, took the bill. "$150!" she cried, "$150 just to tell me my duck is dead!!" The vet shrugged. "I'm sorry. If you'd taken my word for it, the bill would have been $20, but, with the Lab Report and the Cat Scan, it's now $150.00."

~✦~

My pony has a cold. He's a little hoarse.

~♦~

Regardless of whether they were ants, cockroaches, or beetles, he found all bugs to be creepy.

~♦~

One female bee saw her friend dating a handsome human being and whispered to her, "He's a keeper!"

~♦~

I gave her some calamari; she gave me some octopus. We agreed it was a fair squid pro quo.

~♦~

All the waterfowl kept their eyes closed except for one. He was a Peking duck.

~♦~

Two vultures board an airplane, each carrying two dead raccoons. The stewardess looks at them and says, "I'm sorry, gentlemen, only one carrion allowed per passenger."

~♦~

He went horseback riding and never even thought to use the reins, a result of his unbridled enthusiasm.

~♦~

Do animal rights activists prefer PETA bread?

~♦~

Though others had told the producer that the star of the *Mr. Ed Show* wanted to quit, he wouldn't believe it until he heard it straight from the horse's mouth.

~♦~

A dog gave birth to puppies near the road and was cited for littering.

~♦~

Two boll weevils grew up in South Carolina. One went to Hollywood and became a famous actor. The other stayed behind in the cotton fields and never amounted to much. The second one, naturally, became known as the lesser of two weevils.

~♦~

Thanks to fossils, archaeologists have been able to determine that there was once a genetic mutation millions of year ago, causing the creation of a five-legged dinosaur.

As far as we know, this is the first evidence we have ever seen of a reptile dysfunction.

~♦~

The lady tested positive for Lyme disease and that really ticked her off.

~+~

The Energizer Bunny had to audition for his job and had to pass a difficult battery of tests.

~+~

When Billy Bob entered the rodeo arena, the horses became agitated; their nostrils flared; their eyes widened. That's why Billy Bob had come to be known as the "Broncho Dilator."

~+~

"I spilled Spot Remover on my dog. . . . Now, he's gone."
—Steve Wright

~+~

Biologists have recently produced immortal frogs by removing their vocal cords. They can't croak.

~•~

A toothless termite walked into a tavern and said, "Is the bar tender here?"

~•~

A cat ate some cheese and waited for a mouse with baited breath.

~•~

Horses in the movies only have bit parts.

~•~

When a new hive is done, bees have a house swarming party.

~+~

He bought a donkey because he thought he might get a kick out of it.

~+~

I phoned the zoo, but the lion was busy.

~+~

When a cow gives birth, she not only gives cream but is also de-calf-inated.

~+~

Two attractive female birds were showing off in front of some males. Both had spent two hours at the hairdresser, but it was the curly bird that got the perm.

~♦~

There were three horses on a ship, including a sick bay.

~♦~

The chicken went to the middle of the road. She was going to lay it on the line.

~♦~

After the horse ate all of his hay, he had a baleful look about him.

~♦~

A bird watcher had a mynah problem but with no egrets.

~✦~

Scientists have created a flea from scratch.

~✦~

One grasshopper told another about eating corn. It went in one ear and out the other.

~✦~

Two foxes chasing four rabbits decided to split hares.

~♦~

Lions always take great pride in their families.

~♦~

Male deer have buck teeth.

~♦~

A boy told his parents he wanted to raise goats for a living, but he was only kidding.

~♦~

The first saddle was made without foot pieces, but people thought it might stirrup trouble.

~♦~

The zoology professor said to his students that the bobcats in the cage had a body color that varied from medium-brown to gold-ish to beige-white and, occasionally, is marked with dark brown spots, especially on the limbs. They also have white fur on their chests, bellies, and on the insides of their legs, which are extensions of the chest and belly fur. "Can we see the white fur on their bellies?" the student asked the professor.

"No," said the professor, glancing at the animals laying flat on their bellies, "You see these lynx are disabled."

~+~

How do chickens dance? Chick-to-chick.

~+~

An angry bird landed on a door knob. Then flew off the handle.

~+~

A frog went to get a loan at a bank.

The loan officer's name was Ms. Patty Stack. When the frog told Ms. Stack that he wanted a loan, she asked if he had collateral. He showed her something that, to her, looked like a marble and said, "This is what I have for collateral."

She took it to the bank president and said, "there's a frog out there who wants a loan, and this is what he has for collateral (showing him the marble).

She said, "Do you know what this is, and should I give him the loan?"

The bank president said, "Why, that's a nick knack, Patty Stack; give that frog a loan."

~♦~

One day in the forest, three animals were discussing who among them was the most powerful.

"I am," said the hawk, "because I can fly and swoop down swiftly at my prey."

"That's nothing," said the mountain lion, "Not only am I fleet, but also I have powerful teeth and claws."

"I am the most powerful," said the skunk, "because with a flick of my tail, I can drive off the two of you."

Just then, a huge grizzly bear lumbered out of the forest and settled the debate by eating them all . . . hawk, lion, and stinker.

~♦~

A man is sitting at home one evening when the doorbell rings.

When he answers the door, a six-foot-tall cockroach is standing there.

The cockroach immediately punches him between the eyes and scampers off.

The next evening, the man is sitting at home when the doorbell rings.

When he answers the door, the cockroach is there again.

This time, it punches him, kicks him, and karate chops him before running away.

The third evening, the man is sitting at home when the doorbell rings. When he answers the door, the cockroach is there yet again. It leaps at him and stabs him several times before making off.

The gravely injured man manages to crawl to the telephone and calls 911 for an ambulance. He is rushed to intensive care, and they save his life. The next morning, the doctor is doing his rounds and asks the man what happened.

Our hero describes the six-foot cockroach's attacks, ending with the near-fatal stabbing. The doctor thinks for a moment, and says, "Yes, there is a nasty bug going around."

~✦~

A woman walks into a vet's waiting room. She's dragging a wet rabbit on a leash. The rabbit does not want to be there.

"Sit, Fluffy," she says.

Fluffy glares at her and, sopping wet, jumps up on another customer's lap, getting water all over him.

"I said sit, now there's a good Fluffy," says the woman, slightly embarrassed.

Fluffy, wet already, squats in the middle of the room and urinates.

The woman, mortally embarrassed, shouts, "Fluffy, will you be good?!"

Fluffy then starts a fight with a Doberman and pursues it out of the office. As the woman leaves to go after it, she turns to the rest of the flabbergasted customers and says: "Pardon me, I've just washed my hare and can't do a thing with it!"

☙❧

A skunk fell in the river and
stank to the bottom.

CHAPTER 11

For Children of All Stages

I thought I had made a mistake before, but I was wrong.

~+~

Knock, knock!

Who's there?

Boo.

Boo who?

Don't cry; it's only a knock-knock joke.

~+~

Knock, knock!
Who's there?
Sam and Janet.
Sam and Janet who?
"Sam and Janet Evening . . ."

~♦~

Knock, knock!
Who's there?
Cash!
Cash who?
No, thanks, but I'd like some peanuts.

~♦~

Knock, knock!
Who's there?
Doris!
Doris who?
Doris locked; that's why I'm knocking!

~♦~

Knock, knock!

Who's there?

Butch.

Butch who?

Butch your little arms around me?

~♦~

Knock, knock!

Who's there?

Banana.

Banana who?

Knock, knock.

Who's there?

Banana.

Banana who?

Knock, knock.

Who's there?

Banana.

Banana who?

Knock, knock.

Who's there?

Orange.

Orange who?

Orange you glad I didn't say banana?

~♦~

Tom Swifties:

"Were those excruciating adverbial puns known as Tom Swifties invented by the author of Gulliver's Travels?" asks Tom swiftly.

~♦~

"I'm wearing my wedding ring," said Tom with abandon.

~♦~

"I decided which car to purchase after looking at the pictures," said Tom autobiographically.

~♦~

"It's between my sole and my heel," said Tom archly.

~♦~

"This boat is leaking," said Tom balefully.

~♦~

"I'm losing my hair," Tom bawled.

~✦~

"Sure I can climb cliffs!" Tom bluffed.

~✦~

"It's made the grass wet," said Tom after due consideration.

~✦~

"Let's get married," said Tom engagingly.

~✦~

"I didn't see that French 'No Smoking' sign," fumed Tom defensively.

~+~

"This tuna is excellent," said Tom superficially.

~+~

"We've just brought gold and frankincense," the Magi demurred.

~+~

"I have a split personality," said Tom, being frank.

~+~

"I'm about to hit the golf ball," Tom forewarned.

~+~

"It's just gold leaf," said Tom guiltily.

~+~

I'd like to play Bridge but hate the bidding," Tom said wistfully.

~+~

"I've run out of wool," said Tom, knitting his brow.

~+~

"A million thanks, Monsieur," said Tom mercifully.

~+~

"I want a motorized bicycle," Tom moped.

~+~

"I'm waiting to see the doctor," said Tom patiently.

~+~

"I haven't had any tooth decay yet," said Tom precariously.

~+~

"This is a picture of my new house," said Tom, visibly moved.

~+~

"I'm not a crook," Nixon said resignedly.

~+~

"I'd like some Chinese food," said Tom wantonly.

~+~

"So only one person arrived at the party before I did?" Tom second-guessed.

~+~

"Who's your favorite operatic tenor?" Tom asked placidly.

~+~

"How long will I have to wait for a table?" asked Tom unreservedly.

~♦~

"I'm concerned about the number of people not attending," said Tom absentmindedly.

~♦~

"It's a unit of electric current," said Tom amply.

~♦~

"Dorothy, if you're going to Oz again, I'm going with you," Em barked.

~♦~

"I love the novels of D. H. Lawrence," said the lady chattily.

~♦~

"Use your own toothbrush!" Tom bristled.

~♦~

"Don't add too much water," said Tom with great concentration.

~♦~

"I dropped the toothpaste," signaled Tom, crestfallen.

~♦~

"I'll tempt Adam tonight," she said evilly.

~♦~

"This is a good bra," she said upliftingly.

Which president is least guilty? Lincoln: He is in a cent.

~+~

When I was in the supermarket, I saw a man and a woman wrapped in a barcode. I asked: "Are you two an item?"

"Bring me a large helping of vanilla with chocolate sauce," I screamed.

~+~

What did the chimpanzee say when his sister had a baby? Well, I'll be a monkey's uncle.

~+~

What would you get if you crossed a parrot with a centipede? A walkie-talkie.

~✦~

My first job was working in an orange juice factory, but I got canned because I couldn't concentrate.

~✦~

I used to sell computer parts, but then I lost my drive.

~✦~

What do you get if you cross a bullet and a tree with no leaves? A cartridge in a bare tree.

~✦~

Doctors tell us there are over seven million people who are overweight. These, of course, are only round figures.

~✦~

What is the difference between a knight and Santa's reindeer? One slays the dragon and the other is draggin' the sleigh.

~+~

What Disney movie is about the tall-tale-telling champ? The Lyin' King.

~+~

Boyfriend: What is your favorite music group?
Girlfriend: I love U2!
Boyfriend: I love you, too, but what is your favorite music group?

~+~

Most people don't know that back in 1912 Hellman's mayonnaise was manufactured in England. In fact, the Titanic was carrying twelve thousand jars of the condiment scheduled for delivery in Vera Cruz, Mexico, which was to be the next port of call for the great ship after New York City. Mexicans were crazy about the stuff.

The Mexican people were eagerly awaiting delivery and were disconsolate ("desperados") at the loss. So much so that they declared a national day of mourning, which they still observe today.

It is known, of course, as Sinko de Mayo.

~+~

Why did the boy put a stamp on the snail he found at the beach?

Because he heard his father preferred snail mail over email.

~+~

Why did the boy bring a stick of butter to the wedding?

He heard you should toast the bride and groom.

~+~

Two cannon balls got married and had BBs.

~+~

They were married by candle-light, but the marriage lasted only a wick.

~+~

I'm reading a book about anti-gravity. It's impossible to put down.

~♦~

He drove his expensive car into a tree and found out how the Mercedes bends.

~♦~

To write with a broken pencil is pointless.

~♦~

Why could Frosty the Snowman see everything?
He had ice in the back of his head!

~♦~

The man who worked at the watch factory was very funny. He stood about all day making faces.

~✦~

Some people say baseball's not important, but, hey, they talk about it in the Bible. You know, "in the biginning . . ."

~✦~

Did you hear the one about the Liberty Bell? Yeah, it cracked me up!

~✦~

Cavewoman's first words to her husband: "Don't just stand there—slay something!"

~♦~

Eve was the first person to eat herself out of house and home.

~♦~

In 1911, the first pill to cure headaches was introduced, but people found it hard to swallow.

~♦~

New magazine for beginning gardeners: "Trowel and Error."

~♦~

The first diet was for people who were thick and tired of it all.

~♦~

When the inventor sold his patent for malted milk, he felt he got a fair shake.

~+~

There was once a cross-eyed teacher who couldn't control his pupils.

~+~

I got a deal on a new computer, and they threw in the operating system to boot.

~+~

What do you get when you cross a snowman with a vampire? . . . Frostbite.

~+~

What do you call a cow with no legs? . . . Ground beef!

~♦~

Q. How do we know that they played cards in the ark?
A. Because Noah sat on the deck.

Daffynitions

Abdication—Giving up on stomach exercises.

~♦~

Anarchy—Exception to the rule.

~♦~

Antiques—Furniture that is too old for poor folks but the right age for rich people.

~♦~

Arbitrator—A cook that leaves Arby's to work at McDonald's.

~+~

Avoidable—What a bullfighter tries to do.

~+~

Bankers—The rooters of all evil.

~+~

Bore —Someone who, when you ask how he is, tells you.

~+~

Buffet dinner—Where the hostess doesn't have enough chairs for everybody.

~+~

Bungee jumping—Suicide with strings attached.

~+~

Cashtration—The act of buying a house, which renders the subject financially impotent for an indefinite period.

~♦~

Class reunion—Where everyone gets together to see who is falling apart.

~♦~

Claustrophobia—The fear of Santa Claus.

~♦~

Committee—A body that keeps minutes and wastes hours.

~♦~

Counterfeiters—Workers who put together kitchen cabinets.

~♦~

Dictionary—The only place where divorce comes before marriage.

~+~

Diplomat—A person who tells you to get lost, and you can't wait to get started.

~+~

Eclipse—What an English barber does for a living.

~+~

Flabbergasted—Reaction to seeing oneself naked in a mirror.

~+~

Footnote—Useless information placed where you can skip it.

~•~

Hanging—A suspended sentence.

~•~

Hangover—The wrath of grapes.

~•~

Hipatitis—Terminal coolness.

~•~

Hunch—A gut feeling you get during lunch.

~•~

Inoculatte—To take coffee intravenously when you are running late.

~+~

Intaxication—Euphoria at getting a tax refund, which lasts until you realize it was your money to start with.

~+~

Karmageddon—It's like when everybody is sending off all these really bad vibes, right? And then, like, the Earth explodes and it's like, a serious bummer.

~+~

Khakis—What you need to start the car in Boston.

~+~

Life—A sexually transmitted terminal disease.

~+~

Locomotive—Insanity plea.

~✦~

Lymph—To walk with a lisp.

~✦~

Osteopornosis—A degenerate disease.

~✦~

Manicurist—Someone who makes money hand over fist.

~✦~

Matricide—Killing yourself on a bed.

~✦~

Optimist—A person who smells smoke and gets out the marshmallows.

~•~

Oyster—A person who sprinkles his conversations with Yiddishisms.

~•~

Pessimist—Someone who looks both ways before crossing a one-way street.

~•~

Pokemon—A Rastafarian proctologist.

~•~

Politician—One who shakes your hand before elections and your confidence after.

~•~

Rectitude—The formal, dignified bearing adopted by proctologists.

~+~

Reintarnation—Coming back to life as a hillbilly.

~+~

Rubberneck—What you do to relax your wife.

~+~

Secret—News you tell to one person at a time.

~+~

Stick—A boomerang that doesn't come back.

~+~

Statistics—Where the truth lies.

~♦~

Subdued—Like, a guy, like, who works on one of those, like, submarines, man.

~♦~

Teenager—One whose hang-ups do not include clothes.

~♦~

Toboggan—Why we go to an auction.

~♦~

Volunteer—Take on work that makes no cents.

⊱✦⊰

"Hanging is too good for a man who makes puns; he should be drawn and quoted."

—Fred Allen

CHAPTER 12

Great Puns in Store

A beauty salon calls itself The Best Little Hair House in Denver.

~✦~

One florist shop calls itself "Florist Gump."

~✦~

Alexander the Grate (fireplace retailer in Belfast, Northern Ireland)

~+~

All Cisterns Go (plumbing service in York, England)

~+~

ArtSea Gallery and Goods (Port Isabel, Texas)

~+~

Ashwipe Chimney Sweeps (Chicago, Illinois)

~+~

Avant-Card (stationery shop in Berkeley, California)

~+~

Beddy Buyz (furniture shop in London)

~+~

Beecher Meat (butcher shop in Beecher, Illinois)

~♦~

Bona Foodie (market in Brighton, England)

~♦~

Fond Ewe Fine Cheeses (Keswick, England)

~♦~

Frame, Set, and Match (picture framing shop in London)

~♦~

Get Plastered! (interior plaster company in San Francisco, California)

~♦~

Get Stuffed (taxidermist in Islington, England)

~•~

Going Pottie (ceramics studio in Dunkeld, Scotland)

~•~

Grate Expectations (chimney and fireplace service in London)

~•~

Haute Dogs & Fat Cats (pet shop in Dallas, Texas)

~•~

Hearty Boys (catering service in Chicago, Illinois)

~•~

Chinese restaurant in Winnipeg, on First Street . . . **Hu's on First!**

~•~

Indiana Bones Temple of Groom (pet grooming service in Simi Valley, California)

~•~

Jamaican Me Crazy ("family fun store" in Haddonfield, New Jersey)

~✦~

Julius Cedar (lumberyard in Saskatoon, Canada)

~✦~

Junk & Disorderly (furniture store in Nottingham, England)

~✦~

Knead to Relax Massage (Traverse City, Michigan)

~✦~

Knit Wit (clothing store in Philadelphia, Pennsylvania)

~✦~

Latte Da Dairy (Flower Mound, Texas)

~♦~

Luna Sea Bed and Breakfast Motel (Cocoa Beach, Florida)

~♦~

Melon Cauli (greengrocer and fruit seller in Birmingham, England)

~♦~

Merry Pop Ins Child Care (Jacksonville, Florida)

~♦~

Millionhairs (dog grooming service in Bath, England)

~♦~

Napoleon Boiler Parts (plumbing supply store in Alton, England)

~♦~

The Old Spokes Home (bicycle shop in Burlington, Vermont)

~♦~

Old Volks Home (Volkswagen service and repair in Richmond, Virginia)

~♦~

Optom-Eyes (optometrist in Colorado Springs, Colorado)

~♦~

Oui Oui Enterprises Ltd. (portable toilet rental service, Chicago, Illinois)

~♦~

Pam-Purred Pets (pet store in Leslie, Michigan)

~♦~

Pane in the Glass (window washing service in Contra Costa, California)

~✦~

Past Caring (antique shop in London)

~✦~

Phydeaux (pet-supply store in Chapel Hill, North Carolina)

~✦~

Prints Charming Photography (Jefferson Hills, Pennsylvania)

~✦~

Reading Lasses (bookshop in Wigtown, Scotland)

~✦~

R. Soles (boot and shoe store in London)

~♦~

Sew Materialistic (fabric store in Brooklyn, New York)

~♦~

Shoebedo Kids Boutique (children's shoe store in Philadelphia, Pennsylvania)

~♦~

Shoenique Shoes (Longmeadow, Massachusetts)

~♦~

Shutopia (shoe store in Bradford, England)

~♦~

Snip Doggy Dog Grooming and Dog Sitting (Altrincham, England)

~+~

Sofa So Good (furniture store in Vancouver, Canada)

~+~

Specs Appeal (optical shop in Glendale, Wisconsin)

~+~

Suite Deal Furnishers (furniture shop in London)

~+~

The Stalk Market (flower shop in Seattle, Washington)

~+~

Tanfastic Tanning Salon (Brookfield, Wisconsin)

~+~

Thistle Do Nicely (souvenir shop in Edinburgh, Scotland)

~*~

Tiecoon (men's clothing store in Dallas, Texas)

~*~

A Time to Kiln (pottery store in Red Bank, New Jersey)

~*~

Vinyl Solutions Unlimited (vinyl supply store in Greensburg, Indiana)

~*~

Wash Up Doc Laundromat (Clifton, Colorado)

~*~

William the Concreter (concrete contractor in Durham, England)

~✦~

Wish You Wash Here (launderette in Coventry, England)

~✦~

Womb to Grow (shop that sells maternity wear and baby gifts in Lichfield, England)

~✦~

Wooden-It-Be-Nice (furniture repair shop in Belvidere, Illinois)

~✦~

Woodfellas Carpentry & Joinery Ltd (Birmingham, England)

~✦~

Wreck-A-Mended Towing and Automotive Repair (Marietta, Georgia)

~+~

You've Got to Be Beading! (bead store in Mystic, Connecticut)

~+~

Cafes, Chip Shops, Coffee Shops, and Restaurants

Aesop's Tables (Greek restaurant in Indianapolis, Indiana)

~+~

Award Wieners (restaurant in Anaheim, California)

~+~

Bean & Gone Café (Auckland, New Zealand)

~+~

Bean Me Up Espresso (coffee shop in Spokane, Washington)

~+~

Brewed Awakening (coffee shop in Berkeley, California)

~+~

Brew Ha Ha (coffee shop in Phoenix, Arizona)

~+~

The Contented Sole (seafood restaurant in West Palm Beach, Florida)

~+~

Crepevine (restaurant in San Francisco, California)

~*~

C U Latte (coffee shop in Brisbane, Australia)

~*~

Cup-A-Cabana (coffee shop in Corvallis, Oregon)

~*~

Custard's Last Stand (ice cream shop in Boulder Dam, Nevada)

~*~

Eat Must Be First (Chinese restaurant in Baltimore, Maryland)

~*~

Edible Complex (restaurant in Portland, Oregon)

~♦~

Edinburger Takeaway (restaurant in Edinburgh, Scotland)

~♦~

En-Thai-Sing (Thai restaurant in Mildenhall, England)

~♦~

Espresso Yourself (coffee shop in Newport, Pennsylvania)

~♦~

The Fat Angel Bakery in Fairfax has a sandwich sign out front that states, "Get your buns in here!"

There's a sod farm just north of Salem, Oregon, that has a sign out front that reads, "We just keep rollin' a lawn!"

~♦~

Fish-cotheque (fish and chips shop in London)

~❖~

For Cod and Ulster (fish and chips shop in Belfast, Northern Ireland)

~❖~

For Cod's Sake (fish and chips shop in Cheltenham, England)

~❖~

Franks A Lot (restaurant in East Dundee, Illinois)

~❖~

Franks for the Memories (restaurant in Mundelein, Illinois)

~❖~

Frying Nemo (fish and chips shop in Goole, England)

~+~

Goodbuy Mr Chips (fish and chips shop in Derby, England)

~+~

Goodfillas (sandwich bar in Bristol, England)

~+~

The Great Impasta (Italian restaurant in Champaign, Illinois)

~+~

Grillers in the Mist (fish restaurant in Katoomba, Australia)

~+~

Higher Grounds Café (coffee shop in Philadelphia, Pennsylvania)

~✦~

Ho-Lee-Chow (Chinese restaurant in Toronto, Canada)

~✦~

Howe's Bayou (Cajun restaurant in Ferndale, Michigan)

~✦~

Jamaican Me Hungry (restaurant in Key West, Florida)

~✦~

Jonathan Livingston Seafood (seafood restaurant in Reykjavik, Iceland)

~✦~

Just Falafs (restaurant in London)

~♦~

Just the Plaice (fish and chips shop in Swanage, England)

~♦~

Kumquat Mae (vegetarian restaurant in Sheffield, England)

~♦~

The Lattetude Bistro (coffee shop in Decatur, Georgia)

~♦~

Lettuce B. Frank (restaurant in Santa Barbara, California)

~♦~

Lettuce Souprise You (restaurant in Atlanta, Georgia)

~•~

Lord of the Fries (restaurant in Melbourne, Australia)

~•~

Gag Reflex (Comedy management in Manchester England)

~•~

American Hair Force (hair salon in Elk Grove, California)

~•~

Barber Blacksheep (hair salon in Brighton, England)

~•~

Combing Attractions Hair Salon (Janesville, Wisconsin)

~✦~

Connecticutz Barber Shop (Groton, Connecticut)

~✦~

Curl Up and Dye (hair salon in Las Vegas, Nevada)

~✦~

Deb 'n' Hair (hair salon in Worcester Park, England)

~✦~

From Hair 2 Eternity (hair salon in New Baden, Illinois)

~✦~

Hairanoya (hair salon in Oakland, California)

~ + ~

Hairaphernalia (hair salon in West Dover, Vermont)

~ + ~

Hairchitects Salon (hair salon in Campbell, California)

~ + ~

The Hair Em (hair salon in Willow Street, Pennsylvania)

~ + ~

Hair Force One (hair salon in Holbrook, New York)

~ + ~

Hairitics Dye For Your Beliefs (hair salon in Chicago)

~ + ~

Hair Me Out (hair salon in San Francisco, California)

~+~

Hair-O-Dynamics (hair salon in Cuba, Missouri)

~+~

Hair Razors (hair salon in Grand Junction, Colorado)

~+~

Bar Humbug (bar and restaurant in Bristol, England)

~+~

Booze Brothers Off License (Preston, England)

~+~

Brews Brothers (bar and night club in Pittston, Pennsylvania)

~✦~

Chez When Cocktail Lounge (Sedalia, Missouri)

~✦~

Lawrence of Oregano Pub (Halifax, Nova Scotia)

~✦~

Pour Judgment (bar in Newport, Rhode Island)

~✦~

Tequila Mockingbird Mexican Bar and Grill (Ocean City, Maryland)

~✦~

U Otter Stop Inn (bar in Minneapolis, Minnesota)

~+~

What Ales You (bar in Burlington, Vermont)

~+~

Fu's Rush Inn (Polynesian restaurant in Hewlett, New York)

~+~

At an optometrist's office: "If you don't see what you're looking for, you've come to the right place."

~+~

There was a pet grooming business on Route 22 in Whitehouse Station, New Jersey, called LaundraMutt.

~•~

A mail-order cheese shop in northeastern Pennsylvania: "Cheeses of Nazareth."

Stir-fry cooks come from all woks of life.

CHAPTER 13

Soup to Nuts

Two cannibals are eating a clown. One says to the other: "Does this taste funny to you?"

~♦~

One part milk of magnesia mixed with one part orange juice and one part vodka makes a Phillips Screwdriver.

~♦~

One part prune juice and one part vodka makes a Pile-driver.

~+~

He believed that his wife's terrible coffee was grounds for a divorce.

~+~

Two peanuts walk into a bar and one is a salted.

~+~

A boiled egg in the morning is hard to beat.

~+~

The fattest knight at King Arthur's round table was Sir Cumference. He acquired his size from too much pi.

~+~

Dijon vu: The same mustard as before.

~♦~

Practice safe eating—always use condiments.

~♦~

Everyone was curious to find out who won the chili contest but the judge refused to spill the beans.

~♦~

It was a cloudless day when they brought out the ice cream, chocolate syrup, and whipped cream, but a few of the guests expected sprinkles.

~♦~

The conscientious dieter always brought home half his pasta because the portions were so large. He figured, "A penne saved is a penne earned."

~♦~

My wife's coffee tastes like dirt, which isn't surprising because it was ground this morning.

~✦~

Ivana Trump married Orson Bean. She then divorced him to marry His Majesty, King Oscar. When she found that royally unsuitable, she moved in film producer Louis B. Mayer. She found the lime too light and left it for her present husband, ex-Congressman Anthony Wiener. You may address her as Ivana Bean Oscar Meyer Wiener.

~✦~

I know some people in Seattle who sell unpasteurized milk on the black market. They have been accused of skimming.

~✦~

"He ate Post Toasties, Cheerios, and Raisin Bran." The comma before the "and" is, of course, a cereal comma.

~✦~

Before his late night flight, the pilot went to his favorite hangout and had a hangar steak.

~+~

Do you know about the electrician who had so much coffee he was completely wired?

~+~

I have never tasted a California pistachio nut worth its salt.

~+~

Can you freeze chili?

~+~

Did you hear about the guy who was hit in the head by a bottle of soda?

Lucky for him, it was a soft drink.

~+~

The late Saddam Hussein's favorite meal was Iraq of Lamb.

~+~

Do you know which foreign mustard offers discounts? Grey Coupon.

~+~

Does a cannibal who eats his parents have an edible complex?

~+~

When she went online to learn to bake a special Indian bread; she was astonished to find that there was a whole chat room devoted to it.

~+~

Here is a story about a famous food critic's recent visit to Europe last summer. He had a delightful time sampling the cuisine in Italy, France, and Germany, but he made the mistake of stopping off in London on the way home. Needless to say, he found English food bland and overcooked. However, one day he had a great meal of fish and chips at a London pub. He asked the manager of the pub if he could have the recipe for the fish and chips.

The manager confessed that he bought his fish and chips from a nearby monastery, and so our critic would have to get the recipe from one of the brothers.

So he quickly ran down the street to the monastery and knocked on the door.

When one of the brothers came to the door, he asked him if he was the "Fish Friar."

The brother replied, "No, I'm the Chip Monk."

~♦~

A psychologist brought together two four-year-olds who had never met each other before and observed them. After a while, one child raised a single finger and the other child responded by getting a few marshmallows. Then the child raised two fingers and the other child found some chocolate. Finally, one of the children raised three fingers and the other child found graham crackers and put them on the kitchen table.

"This is a great breakthrough!" thought the psychologist, arguing that all children were born knowing this type of S'mores Code.

~♦~

There once was this man who applied for a bus driver's job at the county board of education. During the interview, the man was told there was only one bus driver job left, the one that drove the special education bus. The man said he would take the job, but the school official asked that he look at the bus first. They went outside down a row of yellow school buses and at the end was a small van with *Sesame Street* characters painted all over it.

The man was a little reluctant at first, but the official told him all the kids would be at the bus stops and all he had to do was pick them up in the morning and take them home in the evening. The man needed the job badly, so he took it.

The first day on the job, he comes to the bus stop, and there is a little girl standing there who is very fat. She gets on the bus and the driver says, "Hi! What's your name?" The girl replies, "My name is Patty," and takes a seat. He comes to the next stop, and there is another little girl who is fatter than the first. She gets on the bus and the driver asks, "What's your name?" She says, "My name is Patty," then takes a seat by the first girl.

At the next stop, there is a little boy standing there. When he gets on the bus he says, "Hi, I'm Ross, and I'm special." At the next stop, there is another little boy standing there and when asked his name he says, "Hi, I'm Lester Cheatum." Lester takes the seat behind the driver, and pulls off his shoes. He starts picking the loose skin on his bunions and throwing it at the driver. This being the last stop, the driver takes the group of special kids to school.

This same scene happens every day for a week. On Friday, the driver goes into the superintendent's office and says, "I quit! I can't take it anymore!"

When asked why, the driver says, "Every day it's the same thing! Two obese Pattys, special Ross, and Lester Cheatum picking bunions on a *Sesame Street* bus."

~♦~

My brother-in-law talked me into investing in a new brand of ketchup. I probably should never have invested; of course, that's just Heinz-sight.

~♦~

What did the grape say when it got stepped on? Nothing—but it let out a little whine.

~✦~

Selling coffee has its perks.

~✦~

The Mexican chef, living in Australia, prepared reef-dried beans.

~✦~

The rotten bananas were very unappealing.

~✦~

I hadn't planned on having a four-course Indian meal, but I got curried away.

~✦~

Two boys grew up interested in the priesthood: Jimmy James and Johnny Secola.

While both dedicatedly studied the Bible, Johnny Secola was always a little more knowledgeable than Jimmy James. Both boys grew up and followed similar paths. They both became priests, then monsignors, then bishops, and eventually cardinals. Johnny Secola was still the brighter star of the two.

One night, the Pope died in his sleep. The college of cardinals had to decide who among them would be the new pope. Johnny Secola and Jimmy James were now competing to be the head of the church. Johnny thought that he would be a "shoe-in," as he had beaten Jimmy at everything before.

The cardinals held the election, and who won? Jimmy James.

Johnny asked head cardinal in charge of the election what had happened.

The cardinal shook his head wearily and said, "Johnny, I'm sorry. But we really couldn't have the leader of the church have a name like Pope Secola."

~ + ~

I went to a seafood disco last week . . . and pulled a mussel.

~+~

Texas dessert: "Remember the à la mode!"

~+~

A successful diet is the triumph of mind over platter.

~+~

William Tell was not only a great patriot and a great archer, but he was also a great cook.

One day, after he had prepared a new dish for his friends, he said, "I think there are one or more spices missing. What do you think?" Their answer was, "Only thyme, Will Tell!"

~+~

Years ago, there was a baker's assistant whose sole job was to pour the dough mixture for making sausage rolls (apparently the royal family loved sausage). Because people were identified by their professions, he was just called Richard the Pourer.

One day, Richard ran out of some key ingredients, namely a secret spice he used in the batter. He called his apprentice and sent him to the store to buy more spices. When the apprentice arrived at the store, he found that he had forgotten the name of the ingredient. Hoping that the store-keeper might be able to figure it out, he described it to him, "It's for Richard the Pourer for batter for wurst."

~♦~

French porridge would be oat cuisine.

~♦~

Sir Isaac Newton had a theory of how to get the best outcomes in a courtroom. He suggested to lawyers that they should drag their arguments into the late afternoon hours. The English judges of his day would never abandon their four o'clock tea time, and, therefore, would always bring down their hammer and enter a hasty, positive decision so they could retire to their chambers for a cup of Earl Grey.

This tactic used by the British lawyers is still recalled as Newton's Law of Gavel Tea.

⁂

The scuba diving student was in over his head.

CHAPTER 14

Miscellaneous

She loved being married to her husband, and it was the only cause she ever espoused.

~+~

He chose to live in the hills of Odessa because he could no longer climb steppes.

~+~

Is it true that college students can only buy term insurance?

~•~

Humpty Dumpty started becoming lethargic in the spring. By summer, he was in clinical depression, and we could almost predict he was going to have a bad fall.

~•~

He was a hard-driving writer who wrote ten hours a day, but he also made a lot of mistakes. Doctors now refer to this patient as a good example of a "Typo" personality.

~•~

Are Jews buried in a matzohleum?

~•~

Cocaine isn't all that it's cracked up to be.

~•~

Every town in Wyoming seemed uninhabited. Even Casper seemed like a ghost town.

~+~

She was disapproving of all of her sorority sisters and eventually dubbed "The Sweetheart of Stigmafy."

~+~

She knew she felt much better after each acupuncture treatment, but she couldn't pinpoint why.

~+~

His doctor told the Chinese businessman that he was working too hard and might indeed have a "Taipei Personality."

~✦~

The therapist reported that his patient planned a trip to the Arctic Circle and then changed her mind and wanted to visit Antarctica. She did this repeatedly. Finally he diagnoses her as being Bi-Polar.

~✦~

My friend said that he loved multiplication. I replied, "That goes double for me."

~✦~

When the maternity nurses started taking more and more time off, the hospital administrators recognized that the nurses were going through a midwife crisis.

~✦~

The fountain of youth was just a Ponce scheme.

~✦~

The thieves stole more than one thousand cases of soap and proceeded to make a clean getaway.

~✦~

A thief who stole a calendar got twelve months.

~✦~

What do you call an arrogant fugitive falling from a building? Condescending.

~✦~

Prison walls are never built to scale.

~✦~

When the man was shot with a BB gun, the case ended up in a pellet court.

~♦~

Crackle and Pop had gained a measure of independence from their coworker, so when they decided to retire, it wasn't a Snap decision.

~♦~

The Unabomber's brother once described his brother as having a short fuse.

~♦~

My former girlfriend wrote to tell me she had gone through an ordination ceremony to become a female priest but feared that the Vatican might retaliate—at least that's what my ex communicated.

~♦~

Absinthe makes the heart grow fonder.

~•~

Late in life, when Saul Bellow was offered a teaching position in New England, the University of Chicago made every effort to keep him the Loop.

~•~

The computer consultant didn't declare his income because it was a cache business.

~•~

My Indian friend had made me hash brownies but never an assortment of grass-laced breads, which he called his pot poori.

~•~

When Bob's children begged repeatedly for stories about surviving the strong winds of Hurricane Irene, Bob would regale them with his experiences.

~+~

Since Ted spent his childhood in a room in the basement built to protect the family against nuclear attacks, he felt he had lived a sheltered life.

~+~

Does the minister's cow produce pastorized milk?

~+~

Two antennas met on a roof, fell in love, and got married. Theceremony wasn't much, but the reception was excellent.

~+~

The poet had written better poems, but he'd also written verse.

~✦~

When the cannibals deposed and devoured their king, they were playing "swallow the leader."

~✦~

The problem started after the politicians had a Champagne reception at the opening of the new interstate highway and a couple of them had one for the road.

~✦~

A man rushed into a busy doctor's office and shouted, "Doctor! Doctor! I think I'm shrinking!" The doctor calmly responded, "Now, settle down. You'll just have to be a little patient."

~✦~

A thief broke into the local police station and stole all the toilets and urinals, leaving no clues.

A spokesperson was quoted as saying, "We have absolutely nothing to go on."

~♦~

A famous Viking explorer returned home from a voyage and found his name missing from the town register. His wife insisted on complaining to the local civic official, who apologized profusely, saying, "I must have taken Leif off my census."

~♦~

You know why it's always cool at San Francisco baseball games? All those giant fans.

~♦~

What's Irish and stays out all night? Patio furniture.

~♦~

Review of the play, "I Am a Camera": "No Leica."

—Goodman Ace

~∗~

Local Area Network in Australia: The LAN down under.

~∗~

The harm caused by sibling rivalry is relative.

~∗~

When my father left on vacation, he told me to study the Spanish word for city. I responded, "I'll ciudad."

~∗~

Two young men were out in the woods on a camping trip when they came upon this great trout brook. They stayed there all day, enjoying the fishing, which was super.

At the end of the day, knowing that they would be graduating from college soon, they vowed that they would meet in twenty years at the same place and renew the experience.

Twenty years later, they met and traveled to a spot near where they had been years before. One of the men said to the other, "This is the place!"

The other replied, "No, it's not!"

The first man said, "Yes, I recognize the clover growing on the bank on the other side. To which the other man replied, "Silly, you can't tell a brook by its clover."

~✦~

Two podiatrists became arch rivals.

~✦~

There is some Confucian about the oldest religion in China.

~✦~

Nylon stockings give women a run for their money.

~+~

Is a book on voyeurism a peeping tome?

~+~

The shareholders of a compass manufacturer were concerned that the company wasn't heading in the right direction.

~+~

When the lights went out, Leroy re-fused to put the power back on.

~+~

What do you call a sports car made of wood? A Lumber-ghini.

~+~

I couldn't believe that the statue was not made of stone. Next time, I won't take a work of art for granite.

~+~

Help! The supply of pants is being depleated.

~+~

The gay fellow wished to visit the night club. He would need a mandate to do so.

~+~

Record two television shows at the same time? Why, that's not even remotely possible.

~+~

I don't know why my friend insisted on taking the late test without wearing any cosmetics. Everyone knew that it was a makeup exam.

~+~

Teddy Roosevelt was a bit distrusting of big business.

~•~

It was such a lovely day I thought I'd go walking down by the seashore.

As I was walking, I began to count the slits in the boardwalk, one, two, three . . . And then a policeman asked what I was doing.

I said, "Hello, officer. It's such a lovely day I thought I'd just take a stroll down by the shore and count the slits in the boardwalk."

He says, "I think I'll join you. All the bad guys are locked up, and I'm free for a while."

And together we walked and counted the slits in the boardwalk, 17, 18, 19 . . .

And as we passed a man standing by the railing, he asked what we were doing.

He said he was a doctor and said he, too, would join us. And we continued on and counted the slits in the boardwalk, 36, 37, 38 . . .

There was a woman walking her dog who asked what we were doing. After I told her, she insisted on walking with us and counting the slits in the boardwalk, 56, 57, 58 . . .

Then a mail-lady passed by. She, too, thought it was a lovely day, and, as she had already delivered her mail, she also wanted to take a nice stroll along the seashore and help us count the slits in the boardwalk, 87, 88, 89 . . .

After we walked for about thirty minutes counting the slits in the boardwalk, 178, 179, 180 . . . , Suddenly, as no one was paying attention, everyone walked right off and fell into the water.

And the moral of the story is: "When you're out of slits, you're out of pier."

~ ♦ ~

"A pessimist looks at the world through morose-colored glasses."

—Rebecca Boroson

~ ♦ ~

"Every dogma must have its day."

—Carolyn Wells

~ ♦ ~

"A fool and her money are soon courted."

—Helen Rowland

~✦~

"One man's Mede is another man's Persian."

—George S. Kaufman

~✦~

As the gardener said when asked why he was cutting grass with a pair of scissors: "That's all there is; there isn't any mower."

~✦~

Sydney Smith, observing two women bawling at each other across a backyard, noted that they would never be able to agree because they were arguing from different premises.

~✦~

Does a phrase like "I'm a sap for tree jokes" make you want to needle the speaker or pine for more?

~ ♦ ~

Why was Cinderella such a bad basketball player?
She had a pumpkin for a coach.

~ ♦ ~

Q: What's a pig's favorite television game show?
A: Squeal of Fortune.

~ ♦ ~

Traveling on a flying carpet is a rugged experience.

~ ♦ ~

Customer to book store owner: "I'd like to return this book on modern medical procedures."

Owner: "Is there something wrong with it?"

Customer: "Someone removed the appendix."

~+~

The policeman couldn't believe his eyes when he saw a woman drive past him on the freeway, busily knitting. Quickly, he pulled alongside the vehicle, rolled down his window, and shouted, "Pull over!"

"No," the women yelled back cheerfully, "Socks!"

~+~

I was in the waiting room of my doctor's office the other day when the doctor started yelling, "Typhoid! Tetanus! Measles!" I went up to the nurse and asked her what was going on. She told me that the doctor liked to call the shots around here.

~+~

I tried to answer my wife's questions about how craps is played, but after a while, I just thought: "What's the point?"

~✦~

The floods washed away a large chain store and most of the employees wanted to resign, but they found out that it's difficult to quit a moving Target.

~✦~

Secco and Vanzetti—the name of revolutionary Italian dry wine.

~✦~

Are female bank officers required to wear platform shoes?

~✦~

Joan knitted a sweater for a boy she liked, but she was too shy to put her name on the gift. The young man assumed it was from a different woman. This proves the adage: "If you sew something, say something."

~♦~

During the days of the Vikings, it was customary to name the first-born males Leif. When the wife of one Viking ruler wanted to give her new son another name, her husband refused, saying, "Into each reign, a little Leif must fall!"

~♦~

I walked out of my house and was immediately hit in the head with a slice of ham. That was followed by a pound of ground beef, then a couple of rashers of bacon. I called 911 and reported what happened. They said, "Of course, we're having meatier showers."

~♦~

A new medical facility with several different specialists opened in a trendy part of the city. Wanting to be different and creative, the administration decided that each doctor's office door would, in some way, be representative of his practice. So, when construction was complete, the eye doctor's door had a peep hole, the orthopedist's door had a broken hinge, the psychiatrist's door was painted all kinds of crazy colors, and the proctologist's door was left open—just a crack.

~♦~

A married couple was having a disagreement while sitting in bed. The wife said to her husband, "You're impossible." The husband replied, "No. I'm next to impossible."

~♦~

Everyone at the company I worked for dressed up for Halloween. One fellow's costume stumped us. He simply wore slacks and a white t-shirt with a large 98.6 printed across the front in glitter. When someone finally asked what he was supposed to be, he replied, "I'm a temp."

~ * ~

I know a man who couldn't stop chewing his fingernails. Eventually, he threw up his hands.

~ * ~

A pessimist's blood type is always B negative.

~ * ~

There was a new preacher who wanted to rent a house in the country. The only house available was rumored to be haunted. Since the preacher didn't believe in such things, he rented it.

It wasn't long before the ghost made its appearance. The preacher told his friends about the ghost, but they didn't believe him. They told him the only way they would believe was if he would take a picture of the ghost.

The preacher went home and called for the ghost. When it appeared, the preacher explained the situation and asked the ghost if it would mind having its picture taken. The ghost agreed.

When the picture was developed, the ghost wasn't visible. Feeling very disappointed, the preacher called again for the ghost. When it appeared, the preacher showed it the picture and wanted to know why the ghost wasn't in it.

The ghost thought a minute and replied, "Well, I guess the spirit was willing, but the flash was weak."

~+~

A farmer told me he has 200 head of cattle. He thought there were only 196 until he rounded them up.

~+~

Quasimodo goes to a doctor for his annual checkup. "I think something is wrong with your back," the doctor says. "What makes you say that?" Quasimodo asks. "Oh," the doctor replies. "It's just a hunch.

~+~

Back in the 1800s, the Tates Watch Company of Massachusetts wanted to produce other products, and since they already made the cases for watches, they used them to produce compasses. The new compasses were so bad that people often ended up in Canada or Mexico rather than California. This, of course, is the origin of the expression, "He who has a Tates is lost!"

~+~

The fairy Tinker Bell hoped to be Peter Pan's companion, but he rejected her for the more mundane Wendy.

Devastated by this downturn of events, Tinker Bell decided to get as far away from Never-Never Land as she could. Her flight from fantasy land ended in Fresno, California, where she became a waitress at a roadside truckstop.

One day, an especially rowdy group of truckers came into the restaurant.

They got roaring drunk, spoke loudly and rudely, slopped chunks of food all over the table and floor, and left Tinker Bell a measly quarter gratuity per trucker.

The enraged sprite literally flew into a tantrum, pointed to one of the paltry coins, and screamed, "It's the wrong way to tip a fairy who's a long way from home!"

~*~

A hungry lion was roaming through the jungle looking for something to eat. He came across two men. One was sitting under a tree and reading a book; the other was typing away on his typewriter. The lion quickly pounced on the man reading the book and devoured him. Even the king of the jungle knows that reader's digest and writer's cramp.

~*~

A sailor was caught AWOL as he tried to sneak on board his ship at about 3:00 AM. The chief petty officer spied him and ordered the sailor to stop. Upon hearing the sailor's lame explanation for his tardiness, the officer ordered the sailor, "Take this broom and sweep every link on this anchor chain by morning or it's the brig for you!"

The sailor went to pick up the broom and commence performing his charge. As he began to sweep, a tern landed on the broom handle. The sailor yelled at the bird to leave, but it didn't. The lad picked the tern off the broom handle, giving the bird a toss. The bird left, only to return and alight once again on the broom handle. The sailor went through the same routine all over again, with the same result. He couldn't get any cleaning done because he could only sweep at the chain once or twice before the blasted bird returned. When morning came so did the chief petty officer to check up on his wayward sailor.

"What in the world have you been doing all night, sleeping on the job? This chain is no cleaner than when you started! What have you to say for yourself, sailor?" barked the chief.

"Honest, chief," came the reply, "I tossed a tern all night and couldn't sweep a link!"

~✦~

Two sea monsters were swimming around in the ocean, looking for something to do. They came up underneath a ship that was hauling potatoes. Bob, the first sea monster, swam underneath the ship, tipped it over, and ate everything on the ship.

A little while later, they came up to another ship, also hauling potatoes. Bob again capsized the ship and ate it all.

The third ship they found was also hauling potatoes, and Bob once again capsized it and ate the entire thing.

Finally, his buddy, Bill, asked him, "Why do you keep tipping over those ships full of potatoes and eating everything on board?" Bob replied, "I just can't help myself once I start. Everyone knows you can't eat just one potato ship."

~◆~

A panda walked into a restaurant and ordered a big meal. After eating it, he took out a pistol and put four shots into the ceiling and began to leave.

The manager ran up and demanded: "What are you doing, shooting up my restaurant and trying to leave without paying?"

The panda answered indignantly: "I am a panda!"

"So?" replied the manager.

"Just look it up," said the panda.

They got an encyclopedia and looked up "panda." Sure enough, there it was. It said: "Panda, a large bearlike animal of Asia that eats shoots and leaves."

~ ∗ ~

A father created a scavenger hunt for his children to keep them occupied one summer. To make it tougher, he put all the names of the items into riddles and clues. One of his boys was adept at figuring out these clues and had gathered all the items, save one. He approached his father and said, "I believe I have everything, but there is one clue of which I'm unsure. Can you tell me, what is the answer to the final clue 'two bees'?"

His father replied, "I cannot say. But I will tell you this, two bees, or not two bees, that is the quest, son."

~✦~

A man bought a sports car that was so close to the ground that it could pass under the bar at toll booths. Though the temptation was great, he avoided it until late one night, when he zoomed through underneath the bar. The resulting alarm swiftly produced a state trooper, who demanded the driver's license and registration.

"What did I do?" asked the man. Replied the trooper, "Never send to know for whom the toll bells. It bells for thee."

~✦~

Among Mary Conrad's many talents was flying planes and on one particular day she was flying herself and another woman, Grace Wilson, across the mountains in her plane. A winter storm struck suddenly, and the plane crashed. Mary suffered a broken leg and many lacerations and bruises, and Grace did not survive. Even after the storm stopped, Mary could not get out of the mountains, and she had little in the way of provisions.

After several days, she was faced with the difficult choice of starving to death or obtaining nourishment from the other woman's body, which had been preserved by the cold. When Mary was found alive a week later, she did not conceal what she'd done on the mountain, reasoning that it was better to get the publicity over with immediately. The media treated her cautiously, but rather sympathetically, except for one headline writer, who could not resist the front page declaration, "Hale Mary, Full of Grace."

~+~

Maria Navratilova upon defecting to the United States: "Do you cache Czechs?"